Un·scripted

Un·scripted

How Women Holding It All Together—at
Home, at Work, and Inside—Can Start
Choosing Themselves Again

Melissa Churchard Hannon
Executive Coach and
Leadership Development Facilitator

"If you're not home
to make a hot meal,
somebody else
will be"

Introduction

In 2015 when I led a training for women working at a global engineering company, I didn't expect to hear the words *blow job*.

One woman at the training, Alisa, worked on the design team in charge of developing a new robot. On a team of five men, she was the only female. Unfortunately that ratio represented much of the company—and industry.

Alisa shared that she was constantly engaging with a good ole boys' club that wasn't exceptionally comfortable with the idea of a woman hanging around. She was stuck on the outside looking in as the group collectively agreed the robot's name would be The Bitch. Alisa had worked hard to get her position on that design team, and she loved the work enough that she didn't say anything for fear of *also* being labeled a bitch. As you can imagine, things quickly got worse.

During testing, each time the robot did something positive, it was labeled a "blow job" or an "excellent lay." If it failed to do something it was supposed to, it was deemed a failure—aka "taking it up the ass." On the robot's worst days, it was a "whore."

When Alisa finally spoke up and said she was uncomfortable with these wildly offensive and misogynistic descriptions, the men laughed and told her she was too sensitive—a common way for men to dismiss women's concerns.

This is an extreme example. But it's a story that perfectly depicts the concept that I'll spend the rest of this book diving into: The social generational default for women.

In Chapter 1, I'll explain more about what this means. But in short, the social generational default is the messaging, both implicit and explicit, that we receive as women from the time we're born through adulthood. It includes both the messages we receive from our families about how to be a "good girl," as well as the input we receive from larger society about how a woman "should" behave.

Women are supposed to be quiet, calm, and demure, even when they're mistreated and face sexist microaggressions—or just plain aggression. Don't make a scene. Don't cry or be too emotional. Don't be dramatic. And definitely don't get "hysterical."

This default often keeps us stuck both in our careers and personal lives. It often leaves women feeling frustrated, angry, stressed, and alone.

The alternative to the social generational default—and what this book will teach you—is how to put conscious choice into action. In other words, actively rewriting the script you've been handed, safely pushing back against gender stereotypes and expectations, and developing a more equitable reality.

The first half of this book will outline what these concepts (social generational default and conscious choice) are, how they form, and how women can recognize when they're locked into a default expectation. Of course men also face their own gendered expectations and default behaviors pushed upon them by society and how they are raised. That could be a book of its own. But in this one, we'll focus only on the default expectations of women and how they can craft a new reality. You'll hear personal stories from a compilation of my current and past clients, and read some of the research and data around these concepts.

In the second half of the book, I'll outline my four-step process—the ALIGN framework—to begin shedding your own social generational default, pursue your unique version of conscious choice, and craft a life and career that feels right to *you*.

This four-step process has been decades in the making. I've faced my own hurdles related to the social generational default, as well as coached other women on how to pursue more conscious choices in their own careers. I've worked in leadership development since 1993, and I earned my executive coaching certification in 2012. But hearing about The Bitch robot made me realize I wanted to hone in on the unique path of women in male-dominated industries.

The 2015 training session at Alisa's company was one of the sparks that led to me designing this process. I was furious on Alisa's behalf. Those situations do not have to be the permanent reality for women in male-dominated industries. And while I alone (or you alone, or anyone alone), can't unwind centuries' worth of a patriarchal society, what I *can* do is teach women more tools and strategies to face those challenges, figure out where they have agency to change the situation, and work together to write a *new* script for women in the workplace, the world, and in their own minds.

If you feel like you're constantly following the carrot of "having it all" (but never seeming to get there), this book is for you. If you feel stressed, overwhelmed, and stretching yourself too thin to please everyone around you, this book is for you. If you feel burned-out, isolated, judged, stuck in your career, or disconnected from what you truly desire, this book is for you. If you love your work and feel like you should be "grateful" for the position you've climbed to, but something still feels wrong, this book is for you.

Even if you *don't* struggle with these particular feelings, but want to better understand the women in your life who are trying to carve their own paths in male-dominated fields, this book is still for you.

A Note on the Language and Characters in This Book

While this book is geared toward mid-career women in traditionally male-dominated fields, I also want to acknowledge the use of the terms "female" and "women."

Nonbinary and trans individuals have their own unique challenges—and I hope many of the principles in this book can still be helpful in their journeys. The use of the terms "female" and "women" is not to exclude the experiences of those who identify differently. It's simply to put clear language to the idea of gendered socialization.

As a cisgender, straight, able-bodied white woman, I acknowledge both my own privilege and the narrowness of my experience. Throughout this book, I've brought in data and personal stories about women from different races, sexual orientations, socioeconomic backgrounds, and more. Many of my clients and colleagues over the years have been in different demographic buckets from my own. Listening to their stories and challenges has played a significant role in how I developed these strategies—and their experiences, alongside mine, are what this content is built on.

You'll read several personal stories throughout this book. Names and identifying details have been changed to protect privacy. While some stories come directly from a single person, many characters you'll read about are composites, drawing details from various women I've worked with or known. This approach reduces the need to keep up with dozens of characters, while also condensing and elevating the most common issues and challenges women face.

In Chapter 4, you'll also hear from my husband, Mike, with advice for men about how to be better allies in the workplace and at home. Mike and I have spent the last twenty-five years planning and talking through all issues this book unpacks—all while raising four children, launching my business, and growing his teaching and baseball coaching career.

Don't worry, his writing is only around for one section. The rest of the book centers women's stories and perspectives.

To make the most of this book, I invite you to complete the exercises at the end of each chapter. It can be tempting to skim through a book and not engage with the exercises—your to-do list is already long enough! But to get the most out of this content, I strongly suggest clearing some space, even fifteen minutes, to sit quietly, reflect, and begin mapping out your next chapter. You can also find a glossary of key terms at the end of this book.

What This Book Is NOT

Before diving into the specifics for this framework, doing the exercises, or even turning the next page, it's important to recognize one core reality: This content is meant as a **complement to**, not a **replacement for**, systemic change. The burden to end structural bias and sexism should not be on women. Full stop.

However, these steps and strategies to pursue conscious choice and eschew the social generational default are extra tools to have in your toolbox. They'll help you feel less isolated, burned-out, fearful of judgment, frustrated, and out of touch with your core self. By the end of this book, you'll have a game plan for your life and career that will steer you toward more conscious living, more career success (whatever that means to you), more confidence, and more connection to the values that make you who you are.

Most importantly, this book is not a prescription of behavior. There is no right or wrong path. There is only *your chosen path*. This book is about helping you understand your choices and helpful strategies to feel confident in whatever path you pick. Your journey will differ from your sister's, neighbor's, coworker's, daughter's, or friend's journey.

It's critical we support one another and not judge someone's chosen path. The more we can feel confident we've actively and strategically chosen our journeys, the more we can chip away at the social generational default that would try to limit us. With that you can turn the page on the script you've been handed—and write your own.

"Be perfect,
agreeable, utterly
without needs,
happy all the time,
strong and capable."

CHAPTER 1

Unconscious Conformity vs Conscious Choice

"Women should want kids/family and to be a mother."

"Women keep the house clean and organized."

"Be perfect, agreeable, and utterly without needs."

"Show up to work with hair done, makeup on, etc."

"Be skinny."

"You must always be polite."

"If you're not at home to make a hot meal, someone else will be."

This is just a small sampling of what I've heard from women when asked, "What are the messages you received from family and society about being a woman and the expectations attached to that?"

How did we get here? Where do these messages come from? Why are others heaping so many expectations on women? And why do we pile these expectations on *ourselves*?

Most importantly, how do we get out from under the weight?

Shedding that burden can be a lifelong challenge. But that journey has to start with understanding the burden of expectations: Where they come from, how they're reinforced, and how to recognize them in the first place.

Explaining the Social Generational Default

Kristen is the senior manager of a major laboratory. She's in a traditionally male-dominated STEM industry, has a high-powered job, and by every objective measure, is successful in her career.

When we started working together, Kristen didn't feel as successful as she actually was. Instead, her boss made her feel undervalued and incompetent. Deep down, Kirsten *knew* she was good at her job, yet her boss's behavior had slowly but surely eaten away at that confidence.

Kristen's boss, Justin, was the CEO of the laboratory. He was constantly late to meetings (if he didn't cancel them at the last minute). When they did meet, there was never a preset agenda. Without a meeting plan, Justin frequently lobbed random, incredibly specific questions at Kristen—like what percentage of the company's 2022 clients were still clients in March 2024. If she had known he would ask for specific data, it would have been easy enough to look up the answer beforehand and attend the meeting prepared. Instead she constantly felt surprised by Justin's questions and ashamed and embarrassed when she didn't have answers off the top of her head. Justin's loud sighs and not-so-subtle eye rolls certainly didn't help.

On top of this Kristen had been asking monthly for a year about bonuses for her team. They consistently outperformed everyone else in the organization. But whenever she brought it up with Justin, he would make an excuse to dismiss her request. He didn't have time to run the numbers, the board needed to review, or he hadn't spoken with the CFO yet.

This had all gone on for months, and Kristen felt increasingly disrespected and frustrated. Deservedly so! But when I asked her why she hadn't had a direct conversation with Justin about his behavior, she said, "Well, he's who signs my paychecks. I don't want to make him feel bad. I don't want to be annoying. And I don't want to be labeled as a problem—or angry."

Despite Kristen's level of success and her confidence in her ability to do her job, she was wracked with self-doubt regarding *how she presented herself* as a woman in the workplace. Her fear wasn't related to the work of running a laboratory. She feared her boss would see her as an angry, dramatic woman.

This is unconscious conformity in a nutshell. Women are programmed from the time we're children to make ourselves smaller, be demure, not make too much noise, and keep the peace—often at our own expense. Without realizing it, women often take these standards into the workplace with us. And without intentionally choosing that path, or even thinking we have a choice, women often fall into the rut of that prescribed behavior.

Our generational default is passed down to us from previous generations of women. They're the messages you received from your mother, grandmother, or aunts about who and how you're supposed to be, what your responsibilities are (especially around having or raising children), taking care of others, how to keep your home, and how much you should work. However, the messages we ingest also come from the social default: expectations of women communicated to us through advertisements, movies, social media, and more. We're bombarded with messages every minute of every day—from bosses, friends, romantic partners, billboards, TV shows, Instagram, and those *Vogue* articles about how to make a man fall in love with you.

When these two types of messaging—from our families and larger society—combine, I call this concept social generational default. It's the status quo we fall into without even recognizing we've tripped.

Here are just a few examples of where a **social generational default** probably shows up in your life.

Appearance: Wear makeup so you look "put together." But not too much that it's distracting.

Passivity: Be confrontational and you'll be labeled bossy or bitchy. You'll be too "emotional," or worse, "menstrual."

Clothing: Be professional but ladylike! Don't wear anything too revealing. But don't choose anything too masculine either.

Boundaries: Sure, you can have them. But they need to be porous. If someone else needs something, you need to put them first over your own needs. You need to be everything to everyone, all the time. Oh yeah, and if you *do* hold onto your personal boundaries, you'll be weak or needy. You're not supposed to ask for help because that will mean you're incapable of "having it all."

The impossibility of the social generational default for women can be summed up by a bit from comedian Michelle Wolf in her 2017 "Nice Lady" standup comedy special. She says she wants to focus on her career instead of having a baby—only to be told that as a woman, she can "have it all." Why choose one or the other?

"Yeah, stop saying that," she says. "You act like 'all' is good. 'All' does not mean good. You've never left an all-you-can-eat buffet and thought, 'I feel really good about myself. . . . I sure am glad I went back for spare ribs.'"

Then Wolf explains there are too many obstacles in women's way that keep them from "having it all." Here she dives into all the subtle—and not so subtle—messages women receive around deciding whether to have a baby.

"Great, couple things," Wolf says. She speaks slowly at first, listing a few expectations society assigns to mothers. Gradually her voice gets louder, and she builds up into a frantic rush of words—mirroring the nonstop onslaught of messaging women get in the real world.

"We're going to need you to get that car accident of a body back to work as soon as possible because this is America and we don't think you need time to recover," Wolf continues. "Also, you should breastfeed. It's what's best for the baby, but don't do it in public, you pig. Do it in the old janitor's closet underneath the bridge with the rest of the breastfeeding trolls. And don't ask to take time off from work when your kids are sick. We'll think you're not dedicated. Also, why are you such a bad mom? By the way, your salary is just enough to cover the cost of childcare. And we know you're exhausted and you don't really know who you are anymore and you're trying to balance your old life and your new life, but quick! Go have sex with your husband! He's about to leave! He doesn't understand what you're going through! Quick, go now! And, sweetie, smile!"

You don't have to have (or want) kids to understand the joke. Pick anything—your career, your body, your wardrobe—and there's a high likelihood you've been blasted with social generational default programming since you were old enough to understand language. Whether it's the expectation that you'll have children one day, the pressure of "having it all," or the "advice" not to seem too "bossy," this messaging works its way into our bones. It may take years—or a lifetime—to realize it's there.

With all those external expectations swirling in your brain, it's no wonder you have the corner office but still don't speak up to your boss about the fact that you and your entire team are putting in extra effort—all because Jeremy has been underperforming. As a kid, maybe you were scolded for standing up to the boy who tugged on your hair in class. Maybe you directed group projects with a little too much fervor and were labeled "bossy" by teachers. Maybe as you got older, that directness was labeled as "bitchiness."

Naturally, faced with this kind of resistance, you might find it easier to take the path of least resistance. Be more passive, settle down, and stay quiet. Don't rock the boat, because it's not what "nice" women do. (Remember the old nursery rhyme? "Sugar and spice and everything nice. That's what little girls are made of.")

Getting sucked into this tornado of societal or familial messaging is not your fault. You're so busy that it's easy to settle into the groove of the default rather than take the time to pause and consider whether it's really what you want. You effortlessly get caught up in loops of behavior and the expectations placed on you. But life is so hectic that you often don't recognize those loops. As you progress further into your career—and your schedule gets more and more packed—it becomes harder and harder to separate the expectations others place on us and the expectations we want to have of ourselves.

But that's exactly what this book is for. It will help you unwind the messaging and understand what parts of you are habitual (based on the social generational default) and which ones are *truly* who you are and what you want to be.

How to Craft a Better, More Intentional Future

So what is the opposite of this social generational default?

Conscious choice.

Faced with a nonstop slew of messaging about who we're supposed to be, what we're supposed to do, and how often we're supposed to smile, women can walk a different path.

There is a world where you don't have to abide by the social generational default. You can rewind to a fresh slate, choose which beliefs genuinely resonate with you, and make conscious decisions about what kind of woman you want to be—separate from who society expects you to be.

This book is not about telling you which choices to make or assigning "right" and "wrong" to any path. The point is to help you do the following.

1. Recognize there is a choice.
2. Evaluate what works best for you and decide which factors are important to your life and career.
3. Understand the potential consequences or benefits of each path.
4. Walk confidently in your chosen direction and change the path whenever you want.
5. Support and respect the choices other women have made.

How would it feel to be sure that your day-to-day choices are truly yours—not just what you fell into because it's what you were "supposed" to do? What would it look like to be free of the social generational default? Which decisions would you make differently if you weren't worried about how they would look to someone else or if you weren't afraid to disappoint someone?

And crucially, what would you accomplish in your career if you shed the weight of what women are "expected" to do in the workplace—and at home? What if male executives took over company party planning, spearheading the DEI initiatives, and note-taking, so you could focus on your actual job? What conversations could you have? What work could you take on (or drop) if only you weren't bound by other people's beliefs? How would it feel to know you operate from your own set of beliefs—instead of from what others expect of you?

This book will help you answer all those questions. Through research, my work in the corporate world, and personal stories from high-powered women in male-dominated fields, I hope to teach you how to recognize where the social generational default shows up in your life, unpack whether you even want to meet those specific expectations, evaluate the pros and cons of choosing a different path, and look at how to reframe your life and career through *conscious choice* instead of the default setting. You'll also learn how to find the balance between being an integral part of a team and being true to your inner north star.

Let's dive in.

CHAPTER 2

How the Social Generational Default Can Undermine Women's Success

In a perfect—and equitable—world, someone like Kristen from the previous chapter could walk up to her boss and confidently bring up her concerns about his behavior. In that perfect world, her boss would take responsibility, apologize, and appreciate Kristen's honesty and directness.

But if you're a woman in the workplace—any workplace, really—you know that many women don't yet live in that reality.

When we step outside of the social generational default, demand more respect and equity, and speak with a directness that's usually expected only of men, there can be both gains *and* consequences.

On the flip side, though, there are also consequences to sticking with the status quo and playing by the rules and expectations placed upon us. There appear to be repercussions, no matter which path we walk.

This concept is called the "double bind." According to research from University of Michigan's Gerald R. Ford School of Public Policy, women "often face backlash or negative career consequences when they are unable to display both warmth and competence—gendered societal expectations commonly referred to as the 'double bind.'"

The unofficial summary of that research? Damned if you do, damned if you don't.

This book is not about telling you which direction is "right" or "wrong." There is no such thing. Instead, this book is about helping you understand the potential *consequences* and *opportunities* of each path. Whether you stick with the social generational default or do something new, it's important to feel confident about whatever path you choose. To do that, you need to have a full view of the best- and worst-case scenarios. Armed with that information, you can pick your path and stick with it—or recalibrate and turn around on a different one—over and over. The choice and power is yours.

You might think that because the social generational default is the default, there's no harm in staying nestled into that status quo. However, unconscious conformity comes with its own consequences.

These implications can be minor—annoyance, for example. Or they could be much more serious. Unconsciously adapting to the social generational default could keep you stuck in your career, perpetuate harmful stereotypes, or even pit you against other women.

Before diving further into how you can make the best decisions for yourself, your career, and your family, let's first examine the potential harm that the social generational default could cause.

Reinforcing Gender Bias, Roles, and Expectations

Imagine sitting down in a conference room for a meeting with your boss and a handful of coworkers. You're one of only a couple of women there—you might even be the *only* one.

As everyone sits down and the chatter stops, your boss says, "Okay, everyone, let's get started. We just need someone to take notes and collect all the action items. Any volunteers?"

An uncomfortable silence stretches across the room. You notice that many of the men didn't even bring a pen or a laptop. Just their brains.

In this moment, you have two choices.

Option 1: Put an end to the awkward silence, raise your hand, and take notes. You may be rolling your eyes internally, but externally you portray the eager-to-please, doesn't-want-anyone-to-be-uncomfortable female team player. *No one else is going to do this*, you think, . . . *so I guess I will.*

Option 2: Sit in the silence and lean into the discomfort. Taking notes is no more a part of your job description as it is anyone else's. Plus you've noticed that it's *always* a woman who steps up in that silence and volunteers. So you lean back and casually gaze at everyone else around the table until one of your male counterparts raises his hand.

Sometimes, bucking the social generational default can feel viscerally uncomfortable. But saying yes to something you don't want to do solely out of discomfort—rather than intentionality—continues to feed that eager-to-please stereotype that society has saddled on women. But when you intentionally choose a different path, you're helping to craft a more equitable workplace. Maybe in future meetings, there's a certain rotation where someone different takes meeting notes each week, for example. This evens the workload *and* fights back against the stereotype that women are responsible for office housework.

And maybe you're the kind of person who loves taking notes. You have color-coded ink pens, or you've designed a whole organizational system on your iPad. If this is you, by all means volunteer consciously! Keep leaning into your skill set. But if you get a hand cramp and a headache just thinking about trying to organize meeting notes, pause before volunteering out of obligation.

Think about other workplace scenarios when you've taken on something extra just because you felt like you had to (tidying up the break room, cleaning out the fridge, or ordering supplies).

Now consider how often your male coworkers have taken on those responsibilities. Do they feel guilty for not doing these tasks? Do they get in their head about needing to be a better coworker or leader? Probably not.

It's time for you to ditch that guilt too.

And if you truly do *enjoy* ordering those cupcakes for colleagues' birthdays? Keep doing it! The point is that intention should drive more of what's on your plate—not *solely* obligation. We all have to clean our toilets and answer emails. Obligation is just a part of being an adult. But the more that you can trend toward intention, evenly split responsibilities with partners or colleagues, and stop saying "yes" out of guilt, the happier and more fulfilled you'll be.

Departure from Your Personal Values and Loss of Self

When you make decisions from a place of social generational default rather than intention, you risk severing the connection between your daily life and your values. This cord-cutting happens without us even realizing it. And it's a big reason why so many women feel so wrung out and exhausted.

Aria is the perfect example. She had always identified "quality time with family" as one of her core personal values. Her wife and her two teenage daughters are her highest priorities and bring her the most fulfillment.

But as a finance executive, Aria struggled to ensure that the value showed up in her daily life. She was already staring down the stereotypes and expectations of being a woman in a male-dominated field. (While women make up about 46 percent of employees in the finance sector, only 15 percent occupy executive roles.)

On top of that, Aria was working herself down to the bone. She regularly put in 65 hours or more a week. Most days, she set her alarm for 3 a.m. to get a head start on her never-ending to-do list.

The time she *did* have with her family when she was home wasn't exactly quality. In the mornings she would rush out the door, already stressed about what was in her inbox. Then after working all day—and often into the evening—she would return home burned-out and aggravated.

All for what?

Aria wasn't working this many hours because she wanted to or even because it was in her job description to do so. She did it because she felt like she had to. In a male-dominated industry like finance, she already felt "behind." So she defaulted to working twice as hard to prove she was a competent leader. Aria is extremely self-assured, clear and concise with her words, and doesn't use qualifiers like "I think" or "I know I don't have much experience in this area" before she speaks. She knows exactly what she needs to say, and she says it. But that led to her constantly getting feedback that she was too harsh or intimidating. So she put in longer and longer hours, hoping her leadership would be appreciated. But in the process of trying to prove herself, she was eschewing her personal value of family time.

When Aria realized how much she had departed from her core values, she took a step back and looked at the situation with more intention. She decided that a 65-hour-a-week role wasn't for her. And she decided to take on a different role at the organization where she could work less and run a smaller team under a boss Aria knew would appreciate her straightforward approach. A month later she wrote to me and said she was feeling more motivated and driven than ever in her new position—even after one of the toughest experiences of her career. "I feel like my usual self again," she said.

Now not every woman who wants to step outside of the social generational default will choose as dramatic a path as quitting her job or industry. Instead it might mean setting up more boundaries, having tough conversations with a boss, or asking for support from partners or colleagues. It might even mean leaving your job for a better opportunity. All of these can be tactics to retain that connection to your personal values without hurting your career goals.

Constructing Barriers for Other Women

Unconscious conformity to the social generational default doesn't just harm our own individual goals. It also has the potential to harm women as a collective. Unconscious conformity can feed the patriarchal system that's been laid out for us for decades. Is the patriarchal system we live in women's fault? No—but the more we take intentional steps outside of that system rather than settling into the default behaviors, the more we can build a different reality.

This unintentional barrier construction can look like many different things. Maybe you've defaulted to being sweet and docile at work—because you don't want to hear the feedback that you're "difficult to please." But that can perpetuate a reality where difficult conversations are swept under the rug. This ends up harming women more than men in the long run, because in a patriarchal system, men benefit from keeping things as is. To overhaul that system, difficult conversations are often necessary.

This might also be working past 5 p.m., even though you need to go pick up your kids from soccer practice. The social generational default so many of us have been programmed with is some version of "women who have kids aren't as committed to their career." You stay late—and for god's sake, don't talk about your kids too much—because you don't want your coworkers to think you're not committed and capable professionally.

But this sets off a chain reaction, especially for women in leadership positions. Other women in the workplace see you sending emails from home at 10 p.m. and decide they need to do the same. The cycle of burned-out women continues. It also reinforces the double standard we see so often for working parents. As comedian Ali Wong puts it, "It takes so little to be considered a great dad and so little to be considered a shitty mom."

However, if we switch to a more conscious approach, this reality can start to turn. Make the intentional decision to leave when you need to—and women below you on the career ladder will see that it is possible to set boundaries and still do well professionally. This goes for both mothers going to pick up their kids and childfree women who have other commitments outside of work. Meanwhile male coworkers will see women who leave on time *and* still manage to get their work done (*gasp!*). Piece by piece, domino by domino, the stereotype gets broken down.

What About Internal Biases and Self-Sabotage?

Bucking the social generational default means a more intentional approach to your own behavior. But it also means not expecting those same default behaviors of other women. Many people you interact with will make different choices from you—and that's okay. Those different decisions shouldn't serve as ammo for other women's judgments or expectations. We need to support women wherever they are and with whatever choices they make for their own lives and careers.

We all have unconscious biases. The more we can work to recognize them, unpack them, and change them, the more that we can build a future in which all women are treated equally.

Think about all the ways and times when your brain might have had an unconscious reaction to someone based on their weight, age, skin color, accent, education level, or even clothing. Now think about who you had those unspoken thoughts about. Men? Women? I'd hazard a guess that most instant reactions have been targeted at other women.

Unconscious conformity to ideas about how certain groups of women "should" act or be is harmful, especially to women at the intersection of multiple marginalized identities. The social generational default shows up differently for women of color or members of the LGTBQIA+ community or people with disabilities than it does for cisgender, straight, white women. Intentionally stepping outside the default often comes with bigger barriers when you're in another marginalized group.

For generations, women were expected to deal with these behaviors. (Just watch one episode of *Mad Men*.) Women grew up—and are *still* growing—with the social generational default to pick their battles, to not rock the boat, and/or to just grin and bear it.

Stepping outside of that default to ask for a better reality takes a lot of bravery. But it also might result in different consequences depending on your appearance. Let's say the woman thinking about speaking up in this scenario is white. So is the boss. So is most of the company. Speaking up likely won't be easy. But she does have a certain amount of privilege that she can use for good.

On the other hand, if it's a Black woman thinking about saying something to this boss, her calculus might be different. She doesn't want to come across as the "angry Black woman"—an incredibly harmful and still incredibly common stereotype. To her, the consequences of speaking up might actually make her daily life at the office worse than if the boss's sexist comments were to continue.

Regardless of your ethnicity, sexuality, or backstory, we simply can't know all other women's experiences with the social generational default. And we don't always *have* to know, nor do we have the right to know. But we do need to honor and listen to each of those experiences. Imagine the power of standing together ready to support one another, as we all navigate a world in which our roles and expectations have largely been prescribed. Together we can rewrite the script.

According to a 2021 study (conducted by LeanIn.org and McKinsey & Company) called "Women in the Workplace," Black women experience more microaggressions in the workplace than other women, "and are three to four times as likely as white women to be subjected to disrespectful and 'othering' comments and behavior."

One Black woman who participated in the study (and is a senior manager at her company) said, "Someone told me I was 'so articulate.' They thought they were paying me a compliment. It's frustrating to hear those comments, to have your decisions questioned, to be perceived as the angry Black woman."

In the face of this reality, women with certain privileges—whether that's being white, straight, able-bodied, etc.—do hold more of a responsibility to recognize their own biases, speak up against discrimination they see, and push the social generational default forward.

Feminism has long been hindered by its narrow-mindedness. Someone hears the word *feminist*, and they often think of a middle-class, cisgender, straight, white woman. But in the workplace, sexism, racism, ableism, homophobia, and more are inextricably linked. No one gets ahead until we all get ahead. To overcome and move past the social generational default once and for all—and to craft a more equitable future—we have to broaden that view. We have to unpack our own biases. We have to work together to support the collective whole: one person, one workplace, and one community at a time. And wherever we are along the career ladder, we have to keep reaching our hand back to the women behind us—regardless of class, race, sexual orientation, or any other intersecting identities. If not for ourselves, then for the next generation of little girls who will sit at her CEO desk one day.

CHAPTER 3

Conscious Choice

Moving past the old social generational default isn't just about avoiding negative outcomes, such as burnout, loss of self-identity, gender bias, internal bias, stalled career, chronic guilt, perpetuation of gender stereotypes, and unequal partnerships at home.

Conscious choice is also about intentionally—*proactively* creating the future you want. It's about pursuing all the good outcomes that the default holds us back from.

In other words, it's not just about avoiding the stick. There are carrots to chase too.

When women are empowered to make conscious choices about their lives and career—instead of being funneled into the default—a better future is possible.

In the next section, we'll dive into five slices of life and how they manifest differently depending on if you live by the social generational default or by conscious choice. We'll take a look at autonomy/personal values, resilience/confidence, gender stereotypes, professional network/ mentorship, balance at home, allyship/advocacy, and negotiation/salary. For each bucket, you'll read a story about someone who shifted from one side of the spectrum (default) to the other (conscious choice). For each slice, I'll share a quick action step that you can take today to start course-correcting toward more conscious choice in your life.

Autonomy and Alignment with Personal Values

When you take a bird's-eye view of your life and career, do you want it to actually look like *your* life and career? Or do you want it to be a reflection of someone else's belief system and values?

Too often women look up after years, if not decades, of living in the social generational default and wonder, "Is this really it? Is this truly what I want? Whose values have I been living by? Whose expectations have I been chasing?"

When you live by conscious choice instead of that default, you're more likely to answer the first two questions with a resounding "YES" and the last two with "MY OWN."

Social Generational Default
- *Lack of agency*
- *Detachment from personal values*
- *Exhaustion*
- *Lack of clarity around who and how we want to be in the world*

When Dominique and I started working together, she had hit a wall of exhaustion. She consistently worked 65 hours a week, waking up at 4 a.m. most days to get started. She also had two daughters (fourteen and sixteen) who she parented with intention, love, and focus. At work, she had four direct reports, and things were not going smoothly. The company had a long-standing culture of retribution for mistakes, so Dominique's team members didn't trust her to have their backs. Meanwhile Dominique's boss repetitively gave feedback that her communication style was too direct.

No matter how many hours she put in, Dominique felt like she couldn't win. She came home every night even more exhausted than the day before.

> **Conscious Choice**
> - *Autonomy over your path*
> - *Living more closely in alignment with your core values*
> - *Making decisions based on what you want rather what you think others want from you*

Dominique got serious about discovering (and living by) her personal values: family, freedom, and dependability. It turns out her current role had put her on an *opposite track* from these core principles.

Once Dominique got clear on her values, she could reevaluate how her work and life aligned with them.

Family: Within her grind of a schedule, Dominique didn't spend the quantity *or* quality of time she values with her family. Even in her "off" hours, she was so stressed, anxious, and exhausted that it took an extraordinary amount of effort to be present with her family. When she realized how far she'd strayed from this value and how energy consuming it was to maintain the status quo, she knew something had to change. She asked for more help with the kids from her parents and started laying the groundwork for a job transition that would allow her to work fewer hours.

Dependability: Dominique took her team on a two-day retreat to build more transparency and trust. She wanted to prove to her direct reports they could depend on her. In the day-to-day, it was hard to lay this foundation.

Freedom: Dominique realized she had nearly completely given up her freedom in her role. She was tied to a 65-hour-a-week schedule, and her boss's micromanagement style made her feel like she was in a fishbowl. Not very free. With more awareness about her personal values and where she would no longer compromise, Dominique decided to search for a new role that was a better fit. She's now working for a different organization with a culture and values that more closely match her own. This was a risky move, and she and her partner planned ahead and saved extra money to fall back on as she searched. She also worked with a recruiter who committed to keeping her search anonymous until they could find the right job.

Quick Action Step: Pause and do a gut check anytime something feels uncomfortable. If you feel exhausted, take about ten seconds to stop in the moment and ask yourself, "Am I physically tired because I didn't get enough sleep? And am I living this way because I choose to and it gets me closer to my ideal life? Or am I defaulting to someone else's expectations?"

Gender Stereotypes

If there's one thing that women in male-dominated fields run up against nearly every day, it's outdated gender stereotypes—whether a member of the military fighting against the belief that they're physically incapable of heading into battle, an elected official trying to prove she's not "too emotional" to lead the country, or an accountant feeling guilty for not being a stay-at-home mom.

Whether your chosen path falls in line with what's "expected" of women should be up to you. If you want to be a stay-at-home mom because it makes you happy, you should have that freedom. If you want to work part-time after having kids, you should pursue that. If you don't want children at all, you shouldn't have to. If you want to work in aerospace or teaching or construction or art or sports, all those paths should be available to you—regardless of gender and free of judgment from others.

But what we need to avoid is making career—or life—choices based solely on arbitrary, societally-imposed ideas about what women "should" do.

Social Generational Default
- *Women aren't as competent or technical as men*
- *Women lack leadership qualities, are too emotional, and aren't assertive enough*
- *Women are a "distraction" or don't belong in certain work environments*
- *Women will (and should) prioritize family over career*

Megan is a certified badass: plain and simple. She started her career in naval aviation right around the time of the September 11th attacks. After her initial training, she transitioned to her fleet aircraft, the P-3 Orion. She took a yearlong specialized training for the P-3 and then was assigned to her fleet squadron in Maine. After a little over two years flying the P-3, she was selected as an instructor pilot. These are the people who teach flying skills to future military members. (No big deal!)

Megan clearly had the chops. She had the experience. She had the motivation and drive. But none of that stopped her from running smack into outdated gender stereotypes, propagated by the very people in charge of training her.

During the certification process, Megan needed to train alongside two instructors. She had worked with primarily male pilots and other military members her entire career. But this time around, in the cockpit, her commanding officer wouldn't speak directly to her. He wouldn't make eye contact with her. Megan was the only female pilot under his command, and his hostility toward her became so overt that the top training officer had to ban him from flying with Megan.

At this point Megan faced a crossroads: either walk away from a career she desperately wanted because she didn't feel welcome or accepted or keep pushing forward despite some colleagues' biases.

"Experiences like this, particularly in a male-dominated environment like the military, inevitably take their toll," Megan said. "For women aviators, moments like these build up and linger, influencing our decisions and shaping our experiences."

Conscious Choice
- *Pursuing whatever career path matches your skills and interests*
- *Letting go of impossibly high expectations about what you "should" be doing at work and/or at home*

Despite the intense barriers she faced, Megan persisted. She didn't drop out of the certification program. She leaned on her other instructor, who was much more welcoming, for support and guidance. Megan completed the program and is now living her dream as a P-3 instructor pilot.

This was Megan's conscious choice—but persistence in the face of these types of challenges won't be everyone's choice. Some will weigh the downsides (discrimination, being subjected to bullying, feeling uncomfortable at work) alongside the benefits, and simply exit the industry altogether. It's important that everyone chooses whatever will make them the happiest in the end, and for some that will be a different career path. That's okay.

Still, individuals like Megan are important as we head into the next era of gender equity. The more women in positions of leadership or who choose to climb the career ladder in male-dominated industries, the more female role models there will be for the next generation to look up to. Maybe a few years from now in that cockpit, it will be all women.

Each one of those victories is a step towards eliminating harmful, outdated gender stereotypes.

Quick Action Step: Not everyone will fight gender stereotypes by becoming a fighter pilot—and no one should be expected to! But there are always little things we can do to craft a more equitable world. This week, think of one or two tiny ways you can fight back against gender stereotypes. Maybe you ask your partner to do all the grocery shopping. Put your headphones on at the office and don't feel obligated to smile at everyone. Buy a green outfit for your friend's new baby girl. Ignore the messes others leave in your house. Read a book about military equipment. Make it your son's weekly responsibility to fold the laundry. Go to the football game on your own.

Have fun with this! Not every battle against stereotypes has to be a big deal. Sometimes it's just about setting a small, consistent example that women—*and men, and all humans!*—contain multitudes and nobody should be boxed in by claustrophobic stereotypes. When we consciously choose different paths, we stop perpetuating this cycle.

Balance at Home

Practically every woman I come across has struggled with values-driven living. Most are drowning in responsibilities, don't have enough time for the people and things that matter to them, and generally feel like they're not doing *any of it well* enough. In fact, you're likely reading this and thinking to yourself, *Yeah . . . no shit! Work-life balance doesn't exist!*

Not only is "balance" (heavy air quotes!) a common problem across American corporate culture, but women often carry the load of higher expectations at home. Women don't just have to be great at their job and work twice as hard to succeed professionally within the framework of the patriarchy. They're also expected to take on the burden of childcare and housework.

According to the Pew Research Center, in heterosexual marriages, even women who out-earn their husbands take on a bigger share of childcare and housework. In an era where more women are becoming the breadwinners of their households, they're *still* in charge of a more significant chunk of the cooking, cleaning, and childcare. In the US, women still do an average of two hours more work around the house per week than men.

Sounds way too familiar. Women are expected to juggle about fifty balls in the air—then to feel guilty if they drop even one.

Social Generational Default

- *Women are expected to plan and organize family gatherings, holidays, vacations, and social events to ensure everyone stays connected and relationships are nurtured*
- *Women should take on the "nurturer" role in a relationship by prioritizing their spouse's needs and providing emotional support*
- *Women manage household logistics such as meal planning, cleaning, home organization, and remembering schedules (aka the "mental load")*
- *Women are the primary caregivers for children and handle school drop-offs, doctor appointments, emotional support, and more*

Jackie's day-to-day life had started to feel untenable.

She was police chief of a mid-sized city who consistently worked 60 hours a week and was in charge of a team of twenty officers. Some weeks it felt like she barely slept.

On top of that, Jackie came home and took on the burden of work in her house. Her husband, Martin, was a surgeon after all—as important and high-pressure as her work was, he was *saving lives*. He "didn't have time" to vacuum the living room or clean the bathtub. So that left Jackie to take it all on.

But after one particularly stressful week during which one of her top officers left for a job in another state, a spate of car break-ins had swallowed most of her team's resources, and she didn't leave the precinct until after 8 p.m. four days in a row, Jackie was close to a breaking point. That week she got home late Friday night and just wanted to eat a quick, simple dinner and crash into bed. Then she opened the refrigerator. Her head dropped. In the week's chaos, she hadn't gone to the grocery store in days, and the shelves resembled a college student's fridge: a couple of eggs, cans of fizzy water, and some lonely condiment bottles.

Martin had been home for two hours. He'd had a busy week too, but got home early enough to take a short nap on the couch. Jackie couldn't help but feel frustrated that he hadn't taken twenty minutes to go down the street and pick up a few groceries.

Jackie took a deep sigh and pulled out her phone to order Chinese delivery for the third time that week. Meanwhile she couldn't shake the feeling that *something had to give*. She was at a pivotal point in her career, and taking on the burden of seemingly *all* the household work was starting to wear on her. How would she have the energy to keep pushing for her next promotion if she kept spending so many hours taking care of both herself *and* her husband?

> **Conscious Choice**
> - *Clearly define and distribute household and caregiving responsibilities with your partner and/or support system. Treat this as a shared effort, not just "help" from others. (Bonus tip: Eve Rodsky developed a card game called the "Fair Play Deck" that helps you and a partner divide up these responsibilities.)*
> - *Release the expectation of being the "perfect" partner, parent, or homemaker. Accept that things don't have to be done "your way," and done at all is better than perfect.*
> - *If you are financially able, pay for assistance from others (housekeeping, meal delivery, childcare, virtual assistants, etc.). This is not a possibility for everyone, but if you do have some extra money to spend, leverage it. Prioritize efficiency over outdated expectations of "doing it all yourself."*

Over their Friday night takeout dinner, Jackie explained to her husband that she was exhausted and overwhelmed. She needed support in her own home, she said, and they needed to talk about who did what, because at that point, pretty much everything was falling to her. Martin, who had been lost in his own swirl of stress and busyness, hadn't noticed how out of balance things had gotten. But now he could see how tired his wife was, and he wanted to help.

On Saturday afternoon, Jackie went to the wine store and picked one of her and Martin's favorites. They popped the top at the kitchen table that night with a notepad in front of them and began hashing out everything that needed to be done at their house. Pretty quickly, they realized this might be easier than they'd anticipated. Martin actually enjoyed the process of cooking, and he didn't mind the grocery store. Meanwhile Jackie felt much less stressed cleaning up after dinner than making it. In fact, she really didn't mind cleaning at all. But after being at work for ten hours a day and making what felt like a hundred decisions—coming home and having to decide what to cook? Absolutely not.

The pair decided that anything related to food would become Martin's responsibility. Grocery shopping, meal planning, cooking—he would handle all of it. Jackie would take on most of the cleaning, although Martin volunteered for laundry duties. The two also decided on a more equal schedule for walking their Australian shepherd. Jackie was an early riser and enjoyed strolling the neighborhood before heading into the chaos of back-to-back meetings all day. Martin's surgeries were usually in the mornings, and he was more likely to be home earlier in the day. He would start picking up Luna from doggy daycare and walking her in the evenings.

And the landscaping? Forget about it. Neither of them wanted to do it—so they made plans to call that neighborhood teenager who'd asked to mow their lawn for a few bucks a week. They could afford to hire some support.

As the two finalized their list, they realized how easy the division of labor had been once they put a little intention behind it. They'd fallen into a default without even realizing it—until one of them burned out.

Too often women are the ones who get the short end of the stick with that default. And usually that means they're the ones to reach the burnout point. But with a little more conscious effort—and the willingness to ask for and expect support from those with whom we share a home—we can start to turn that story around.

Quick Action Step: If you have a partner at home, set aside an hour this week to create a list of every household task that regularly needs to be done: everything from weekly grocery shopping to cleaning the grout in your shower. Then think about each of your strengths and weaknesses. Run through each line item and start assigning tasks to each person based on their interests and skills—*with an eye toward equitable distribution.* Maybe you absolutely hate washing dishes after a meal, but you find mowing the lawn soothing. Or maybe your partner wants to listen to their favorite podcast and clean the bathroom every Saturday. Whatever distribution works for your dynamic, the important thing here is that there is an intentional distribution. If you have children at home elementary-school age or older, assign chores to them too. They are part of the household.

If you live alone, sit down with yourself and think through the same list of duties. Is there anything you can drop? Could you potentially afford to hire a cleaner once a month to handle some of the deep cleaning you don't have time for? Can you sign up for a meal service to make dinner one less decision you have to make? Just because you don't have a live-in partner does not mean you have to do everything alone.

Professional Network and Mentorship Opportunities

No one can do it all alone.

That rings true for virtually anything you want to accomplish. But it's especially true for women in the workplace. If you want to progress in your career, it's unlikely you'll get there without support from others. Whether it's your peers helping you with that massive project, a boss who promotes you, or a former manager who serves as a reference when you switch companies, we all need a little help.

But too often, especially if you're a woman working in a male-dominated field, networking and mentorship can feel uncomfortable—or downright unhelpful. Maybe you're the only woman at your company, struggling to find someone who relates to your perspective. Maybe you're pushing up against a C-suite full of men who go golfing together on the weekends. Maybe you've found it challenging to find allies at your company willing to say your name when an opportunity arises.

It's not uncommon for women to feel isolated and frustrated when they don't have access to a supportive network. But if you can find the right mentors, it very well could change your entire career trajectory.

Social Generational Default
- *Good ole boys' clubs*
- *Women feeling like they have to work towards promotion on their own without asking for support*
- *Lack of female leaders to ask for advice or guidance*

Bethany is an estimating coordinator at a major construction company on the East Coast. When she first started her career, she worked at a company that assigned mentors to more junior-level employees. On the surface this was good news. Bethany would have a specific person to go to for questions, and it at least seemed like the organization cared about her career advancement.

But she quickly realized that the relationship might be a detriment. First and foremost, the assigned mentor had no interest in mentoring. No one from leadership had consulted with this person before assigning them to Bethany. Second there were no boundaries or expectations around what mentoring at the organization should look like. It was as if everyone had drawn names out of a hat and then went on with their day-to-day. There was no guidance from the company about how often each pair should meet, what they should discuss, how to handle communication, how long the mentorship should last, and more.

Bethany was also the only woman on the operations end of her company at the time. Her mentor had never worked with a woman younger than him, and she was "treated with kid gloves" because of that. After several months—and even being assigned to a different mentor in the company with more of the same results—Bethany was at a loss. She was ambitious, talented, and hungry to learn. But trying to get her assigned mentor to teach her felt like pulling teeth.

Conscious Choice
- *Clarifying exactly what you want out of a mentor relationship*
- *Actively seeking out mentors in the workplace who align with your goals, needs, and communication style and who are are excited about supporting your growth*
- *Asking for help when you need it*
- *Paying it forward: offering your own mentorship to other women lower on the career ladder than you*

If she were going to climb the ladder within her industry, Bethany realized she would have to step outside the box of her company's prescribed mentorship program. Instead of waiting around for a new assignment, she identified someone at the organization whose leadership she admired and went directly to him to ask for help.

This new mentor—let's call him Jamison—was happy to support Bethany. He answered her questions, listened to her curiosity, and stayed late after work to help her learn. He also searched for more opportunities for Bethany to participate in within the company. He advocated for her and some of her peers to be more involved with strategic planning so they could see the "why" behind what they did every day. Most importantly, Bethany knew Jamison would support her behind closed doors, even when no one else was in the room besides other men.

Bethany leveraged this successful mentorship to move up the ladder, eventually taking her current position as estimating coordinator. She's also paying it forward: She joined the Young Professionals Group of her region's chapter of the Associated Builders and Contractors. Now she's set to take over as the group's chair.

As a motivated young professional in a male-dominated industry, Bethany probably would have eventually accomplished her goals. However, relying on the company-directed, status-quo mentorship program wasn't helping her get there. Instead, actively pursuing a mentorship that worked for *her* with people interested in mentoring empowered Bethany to accomplish more in a shorter period of time.

"Mentors who are assigned to you by your company have the potential to be more of a detriment," she said. "There is no harm in finding your own mentor who will help support your growth and development. I'm surrounded by fantastic mentors now in my new role, and it's because they are interested and invested in providing guidance and support to those of us coming up in the industry."

Finding the right mentor can be challenging for anyone—but especially for women in male-dominated industries, where you might push up against good ole' boys clubs. Here are a few tips for how to build your network and find the support you need.

- **Observe your potential mentor's leadership:** Choosing a mentor has to be *intentional* above all else. Take time to pay attention to how potential mentors interact with others. Do they demonstrate empathy, inclusivity, and a commitment to empowering others, especially women and marginalized groups?

Do they have a leadership style you connect with and want to emulate?

- **Be open:** While having a mentor who can relate to your experiences as a woman is valuable, don't limit your search to only women. A male mentor who is an ally and advocate for gender equity can offer valuable perspective and support, especially if you work in a male-dominated industry.
- **Identify your goals and needs:** Before reaching out to any potential mentor, take time to assess your career goals, strengths, potential growth areas, and challenges you face. For example, do you need support with leadership development, navigating workplace politics, or developing a more values-driven approach to your schedule?
- **Be clear about your preferred communication style:** Look for someone whose mentoring style resonates with you. Some people prefer a hands-on, direct approach, while others may want broader advice from a distance. Wherever you fall along that spectrum, be sure to communicate that to your mentor.
- **Outline your expectations:** When you approach a potential mentor, articulate why you admire their career trajectory and how you think their expertise could help you achieve your goals. Be specific about the time commitment you're hoping for and what support you're seeking. A once-a-month in-person meeting? A weekly check-in phone call?

Quick Action Step: Identify two or three people whose leadership you admire. This could be the person in the position you'd like to eventually be promoted to, or someone in a different department with whom you've worked on occasional projects. Be sure to choose someone with traits you want to embody and a position you want to shoot for.

Once you have your targets in mind, ask them if they'd be willing to mentor you. Set out expectations for what you'd want this arrangement to look like—monthly feedback sessions, for example—and explain why you chose them. Chances are they'll want to pay it forward and help out. They were just waiting for you to ask!

Bonus Tip: Regularly assess how your mentor relationship is progressing. Are you achieving your goals? Is the relationship still productive and supportive? If not, it's okay to seek out someone else or adjust expectations.

Better Negotiation Tactics and Higher Salaries

If you've heard this statistic once, you've probably heard it a thousand times. Since the early 2000s, women have earned, on average, between 80 and 83 cents for every dollar a man earns. That gap gets even larger when racial difference are factored in: a Black woman, for example, earns about 70 cents for every dollar a white man makes. That drops to 65 cents for Latine women.

Unfortunately there's still a lot of work to do before we reach equality. In 2023, for the first time in twenty years, the gender wage gap increased. Women's median salaries grew 1.5 percent, while men's increased 3 percent. Several factors play into these trends—many of which women can't control. However, the more women prioritize and improve their salary negotiations, the more pieces we *can* control.

Social Generational Default
- *Men are the "breadwinners"*
- *Secret pay scales*
- *Shame or secrecy around talking about money*
- *Women should be grateful for what they earn and shouldn't be "greedy" by asking for more*

Jasmine had worked at the same nonprofit organization for seven years. She worked with law enforcement agencies and stakeholders to drive better criminal justice policy—and she was excellent at her job. Despite consistently outstanding performance reviews and her years of experience, Jasmine still only received 2 percent pay increases each year. This was hardly a reward for her performance; it wasn't even enough to keep up with the rising cost of living. Still, she was told it was all the nonprofit could afford.

For years Jasmine convinced herself that her other job benefits—like a four-day workweek and the ability to work remotely—superseded her need for more compensation. And she was grateful for her job. She did good, important work in a field she was passionate about. So instead of pushing the boundaries and asking for more, she stayed quiet, put her head down, and kept working.

Conscious Choice
- *Openly, honestly discussing money (especially with other women)*
- *Asking for what you need and want, whether that's a new job title or a raise*
- *Never feeling guilty for negotiating or feeling that you're asking for "too much"*
- *Being proud and clear about your accomplishments and leveraging them for more pay*

Finally, after seven years, Jasmine was ready to consider other offers. If the nonprofit couldn't afford to offer her a better salary, someone else would.

And they did. Jasmine initially received a full-time offer from a company in her field. The only problem? It was 40 hours a week, and she was accustomed to her four-day workweek.

Jasmine was confident in the results she'd gotten at her previous job, and she was equally confident she could drive those results in 32 hours a week. The new company didn't have a single other employee who worked fewer than 40 hours a week. Still, Jasmine put together a proposal highlighting all her accomplishments, skills, and years of experience working four days a week.

After internal leadership discussions, the organization accepted her offer, and Jasmine assumed that meant a cut to the initial salary offer. She expected her next offer letter to be for only 80 percent of the 40-hour-a-week salary, along with 80 percent of the benefits (four weeks of paid leave instead of five, for example).

To Jasmine's shock, when she received the updated formal offer letter, it included the initial negotiated salary and her requested 32-hour workweek.

"Silly and honest" Jasmine (her words!) contacted HR and said there must have been a mistake.

"Nope," the company said. Leadership had meant to offer her the full-time salary while still matching her request for a four-day workweek. And the best part? That final salary number was a 42 percent bump from her previous job.

Jasmine had known exactly what she wanted when searching for a new job, and she didn't hesitate to ask for it. She came prepared with the data and documented results she was responsible for. She proved she was able to do quality work within the schedule that worked *for her*. And she led with honesty and authenticity.

Jasmine could have easily stayed stuck in her previous position for many more years—maybe even her whole career. She could have internalized what the nonprofit claimed she was worth. But instead she bucked that default and consciously pursued the kind of career jump she could get excited about—all while still prioritizing her well-being and her life outside of work.

It's a lesson we can all learn from.

Quick Action Step: Start a running list of all the reasons you deserve that next promotion or salary bump. Grab a pen and a special notebook if you're a journaler or keep a list on your phone's notes app or type everything into a Google doc. The list can include everything from data and metrics to descriptions of skills you have that your team has admired. And remember, speak in the boss's language—the accomplishments should connect directly to business results.

If you're currently a project manager at a construction company but are hoping to make the jump to director of project management or a higher position, here's an example of what your list could look like.

- Helped save the company 14 percent in material costs after streamlining purchasing decisions
- Less than 2 percent turnover on my team in the last five years compared to the company average of 12 percent
- Landed 89 percent of warm-lead contacts, compared to industry average of 64 percent
- Awarded Project Manager of the Year by the corporate office in 2022

Once you sit down and start thinking, you'll be surprised at how many awesome things you've done. Then make it a habit to pull out your list and add another line any time you get another win. When it's time to ask for that next raise, or you're up for a promotion, you don't have to be nervous. You've already done the legwork of documenting your wins. Now it's just time to share them!

CHAPTER 4

How Both Men and Women Can Fight the Social Generational Default

A penis drawn onto the lid of her coffee cup: that was just the beginning of a long string of harassment and sexist behavior that Charise experienced when she started as a police officer in a mid-sized East Coast town.

Charise got into police work for all the right reasons; she was incredibly passionate about helping women in abusive relationships seek justice. She was one of only two women in her department, and she felt every bit of that isolation. Men made sexual comments to her "in jest," then told her she was sensitive when she called them out. They would even go so far as to deliberately place items in her squad car where they wouldn't be found during her routine pre-shift search, and then use that against her later.

Charise was exhausted with the degradation and was equally tired of feeling like she was the only one fighting for herself. When she looked down at her desk and saw the penis drawn onto the lid of her cup—with the tip right at the place where she would take a sip—everyone else laughed. She could either brush it off and try to be "one of the guys" or she could speak up and explain why this behavior isn't okay.

But there's an important third option that's too often overlooked. *Men* could be the ones to step up. Even just one man saying, "Hey, she's right. This is childish and sexist. Keep your penis artwork to yourself," instead of laughing along can make a difference. It's a sad truth, but research has shown that men are more likely to listen to other men. So men who don't want to actively be part of the problem have an obligation to be part of the solution.

This chapter is all about how men can step into that role, along with what women's roles can be in fighting back against gender stereotypes, inequitable workplaces, and the social generational default that tries to tell women to play nice—even when there's a phallus drawn on their coffee cup.

To be clear, sexist behavior and prejudice are *not women's fault.* Ever. But we can take some ownership over how we react to it and how we support other women, and there are strategies we can enact to maximize conscious choice. In this chapter, you'll learn how everyone can play an active, positive part in building more equitable workplaces.

How Women Can Promote More Conscious Choice and Step Outside the Social Generational Default

A massive part of inequality, sexism, and the social generational default lies outside of women's control. We're fighting against entrenched systems largely created by men, and these systems are interwoven with other layers of oppression, from racism to homophobia.

But there are still aspects we can control. The first half of this chapter is all about how to recognize those opportunities and do what you can to prioritize conscious choice.

Stop Shit Talking

You're likely familiar with the "crab" mentality.

When crabs are thrown into a pot of boiling water, they try to escape by climbing on top of each other. Instead of any crabs escaping, this behavior just leads to everyone pulling each other down.

And while a professional workplace isn't going to end up with anyone boiling alive—hopefully—the same mentality applies. As women, pulling each other down doesn't give us a leg up. It just means everyone stays stuck in a negative environment, driven by competition and backstabbing instead of mentorship and allyship.

When women tear down other women, it only perpetuates the social generational default—aka more men in leadership positions and women scrabbling with each other for the scraps.

If you feel tempted to talk badly about a female coworker, pause and ask yourself why. Is this coming from a place of competition? Is that sense of competition helping you *or* her? Or do you have a genuine complaint about this person's behavior? Is there a way to approach her directly instead of talking behind her back? Women make various choices based on a variety of reasons and are all in different places in their mindset. We need to accept all those realities without judgment.

If you *do* decide to talk directly to the person, here are three guiding questions to ensure your feedback is constructive.

1. Is this conversation going to improve the relationship between you?
2. Will this feedback make this person a better employee, peer, or boss?
3. Is the person's behavior having an impact they are unaware of and you can help them by sharing?

Apologize Less

So much of the social generational default is driven by women's belief that they need to keep the peace, avoid conflict, and be "likable." How many times have you listened to your male colleagues discussing a strategy you *know* won't work and haven't spoken up, all because you didn't want to come across as disagreeable?

Or maybe you *did* bring up your concerns about the project. Your male coworkers didn't take the criticism well and said you were being too negative. Was your instinctual next response to say you were sorry? And how often do you think you would get a similar apology from a man if the situation were reversed?

When Priya, a senior product manager at a major tech firm, came to me for coaching, she was constantly apologizing in cross-functional team meetings. Anytime a project was delayed—often due to engineering bottlenecks or shifting executive priorities—Priya would be the one saying, "I'm sorry." She wasn't the one writing the code or changing the launch dates, but somehow, she felt responsible for smoothing things over. Over time, it chipped away at her confidence and authority. She started to believe the delays were a reflection of her leadership.

But Priya didn't have anything to apologize for. In fact, others should have been taking more ownership. The delays weren't hers to own—but because she was the most vocal and the most invested, she became the emotional buffer. What she really needed wasn't to be more accountable, but to stop absorbing blame and start redirecting it where it belonged—with grace, clarity, and professionalism.

It's just one example of women defaulting to apologizing when a more conscious choice would be to clearly communicate what they need. This is difficult, especially if your boss is abrasive or demanding. But the more you can extricate yourself from the instinct to apologize, and the more you can pause in the moment to reflect on whether you've *actually* done something wrong, the more women can all fight back against unrealistic expectations, the default "peacekeeper" role, and an endless cycle of "I'm so sorry."

(By the way, you'll learn more in Chapter 5 about how to integrate a "pause" during tough conversations so you can minimize apologizing, make the most of your response, and live in accordance with your values.)

Release Perfection

Stop. Trying. So. Damn. Hard.

It can seem counterintuitive to encourage women to try *less* when it comes to fighting unconscious conformity. The whole point of conscious choice is that you're *intentionally* clawing yourself out of the social generational default and fighting against the messages we've received since birth.

But part of that default is the expectation of perfection that we often heap onto ourselves. You're not only expected to be perfect in the workplace <u>and</u> keep everyone happy <u>and</u> do your job well. You're also expected to keep your desk organized <u>and</u> keep other coworkers organized <u>and</u> take care of your kids <u>and</u> take on the bulk of housework <u>and</u> stay healthy <u>and</u> dress well <u>and</u> wear makeup so you look put together. *And and and.* When you can release some of those expectations, you'll perform better because you're not so damn stressed. There's also value in separating ourselves from others' expectations and instead prioritizing to make sure we please *ourselves.*

The expectation of perfection extends to the career ladder. By now you've likely heard the statistic—published in Sheryl Sandberg's *Lean In*—that women often wait to apply for a job until they meet 100 percent of the outlined qualifications. Meanwhile men go ahead and apply even if they meet only 60 percent. While new research suggests the gap isn't quite that large, a study from the Government Equalities Office in the UK showed men are still more likely than women to pursue opportunities, even if they don't exhibit all the qualifications.

So what is your role in that gap? Stop trying to be perfect. Double down on your strengths and accomplishments. Recognize that men far more mediocre than you have been promoted since the dawn of time. Even if your car isn't clean, your laundry is piled up, or your hair isn't perfectly curled at the office, you can still do the job as well as—or *better* than—your male colleagues.

End the Cycle of Female Rivalry

There's room for only one woman at the table.

Even if you haven't explicitly been told this, how often has the thought crossed your mind? You see an obvious lack of diversity at your company or within your industry. So when you work alongside another woman, it can feel natural to see her as your competition. The head honchos surely wouldn't promote *both* of you.

It's certainly not your fault for defaulting to this belief. The whole point of unconscious conformity to the social generational default is that it's *unconscious*. But that doesn't mean it has to be permanent. It's time to disrupt those habitual thought patterns.

The truth is that this default can keep you—and your female colleagues—stuck. Instead of seeing your female colleagues as competitors, what would it mean to see them as allies? And what could you do to be a better ally for *them*?

This could be amplifying a female coworker's name when an opportunity arises, or speaking up when you see someone trying to take credit for her idea. Ask the women around you how you can help them. Talk openly with other women about salaries, work conditions, or microaggressions.

And don't worry, this isn't just for you to handle. The following section will dive into what men can do to be better allies too.

What Are Men's Responsibilities for Ending an Inequitable Social Generational Default?

Now it's time to hand this book over to the men in your life: your boss, a close colleague, your partner, or one of your mentors. Go take a coffee break and come back at the end of the chapter.

I'm handing the writing over temporarily to my husband, Mike, for this next section. Mike has twenty-three years of experience as a dad and twenty-five years of experience as a partner open to discussing challenges and opportunities to improve our marriage. He's willing to do things differently, hear me, and divide up all our tasks at home. And he's worked on being a better ally to women for as long as I've known him. He's here to share some of the lessons he's learned and tips for how men can be more accountable and better allies to the women in their lives.

Welcome, Men

If you're reading this, it's because a trusted female colleague, employee, or partner believes you can be part of the solution to the professional gender divide. And remember this isn't just about making workplaces comfier for women. You will benefit too.

Put simply, more gender diversity often equals more successful companies. In fact, McKinsey found that companies with executive teams in the top quartile of gender diversity were 25 percent more likely to have above-average profitability than companies in the fourth quartile.

But none of that comes easily. To build more equitable—and more profitable—workplaces, we need your help.

Here's what you can do to fight back against sexism (at work and at home), give equal opportunity to deserving women, recognize and eliminate problematic behavior (from yourself and your male colleagues), and more.

Speak Up When Other Men Interrupt Female Colleagues or Take Credit for Their Work

One of the most common complaints from women in male-dominated workplaces is the frequency with which they're talked over. And the research confirms this trend.

One study out of George Washington University found that men speaking with women interrupted 33 percent more often than when talking with other men. At Northwestern Pritzker School of Law, researchers found that in a period of fifteen years of Supreme Court oral arguments, female justices being interrupted accounted for 32 percent of all interruptions—compared to 4 percent total for female justices doing the interrupting.

We've all watched this happen, from conversations at bars to workplace meetings to even presidential debate stages. Former Vice President Kamala Harris famously lit into former Vice President Mike

Pence during their 2020 debate when he consistently talked over her.

"Mr. Vice President, I'm speaking," Harris said, smiling across the stage That phrase eventually made it to internet memes and T-shirts because women viscerally connected with the situation of being at the absolute top of their career, trying to communicate their viewpoint, and still being interrupted by men.

So what can you do?

Be aware when you interrupt women in the workplace. A good rule of thumb is that if someone is sharing an idea or giving a presentation, wait until they're done before you butt in with comments. It sounds so simple, but it's (clearly) more difficult in practice. We know you're excited to share your perspective or ideas or reactions. But being patient can create a more comfortable and more streamlined experience for everyone, and thus more productivity because everyone can have their voices and ideas heard, considered, valued, and respected.

But your role doesn't just include reining in yourself. Watch out for when your male colleagues butt in too. Be the one to step up and say, "Hey, Gary, can you hold off for a sec? Lucia is still speaking."

All it takes is one sentence to start shifting the culture and opening up the floor to everyone trying to communicate a good idea.

Educate Yourself About Microaggressions and Call Them Out

The robot story from the beginning of this book? It was a pretty aggressive example of poor workplace behavior from men. Not every bad behavior, though, is so blatantly obvious. Women are accustomed to more subtle microaggressions: statements or actions that reflect either indirect or even unintentional discrimination. As small as these behaviors might seem, the impact can add up fast and that can create a workplace that ranges anywhere from uncomfortable to miserable for women.

As a man it's your job to learn what constitutes a microaggression, recognize these behaviors, and stop them at the source. And remember that if you participate in these behaviors, it's not because you're a bad person or intentionally discriminating against anyone. Sometimes you haven't thought deeply about a statement's impact or you don't even realize you're doing it. Awareness, then, is the first step. Here are some common microaggressions men may not even realize we're committing.

- **Calling women pet names at work:** "Babe," "sweetie," "honey," or "dear" may all be endearing things to call your wife, girlfriend, or daughter. In a home setting, these terms can be affectionate. But in the workplace? Not so much. Women mostly find them inappropriate, condescending, or patronizing. Avoid these terms when addressing women and call out men who use them.

- **Viewing male leadership qualities as negatives in women:** A study that looked at promotion negotiations from both men and women found that women are 30 percent more likely to receive feedback that they're "bossy," "too aggressive," or "intimidating" compared to men. Meanwhile male leaders are more likely to be described as "promising," "knowledgeable," and "sensible." It's time to be aware of the language we use to describe women and their leadership. Would you ever say that your male colleague was bossy? When was the last time your instant reaction to a confident, level-headed woman was that she was too high-strung or aggressive? It's okay to admit if you have—this is the social generational default at play. The point is to recognize those gut reactions when we have them, then course correct to make sure we're providing equitable feedback and not making snap judgments based on gendered expectations.

- **Benevolent sexism:** Have you ever heard a man tell a woman in the workplace that she shouldn't have to shoulder so much stress or do such a challenging job? Would a man tell another man the same thing? How about a boss telling a female employee who's new mom that she should go home early so she can take care of her kid? Would that same directive be suggested to a new dad? In 1996 Peter Glick and Susan Fiske coined the term "benevolent sexism." They concluded these types of comments imply women are "weak, sensitive creatures that need to be protected." When men think this way, they're less likely to give female employees candid, constructive feedback or offer them challenging projects to help them grow. But as we all know, performance-based feedback and challenging assignments are critical for everyone's advancement.

- **Overstepping physical boundaries:** Many men think it's appropriate and even polite to put their hand on a woman's lower back as they pass by. But without consent, this can often make women feel uncomfortable—not to mention it's not something you would ever do to another man in the workplace, right? The best advice to avoid this microaggression is also the simplest: be completely hands-off with your coworkers. Give them space when they walk by. Be aware of "manspreading" (sitting with your legs wide apart) or failing to make room for others when walking down a hallway. These are all examples of invasion of space.

- **Asking a woman why she's not smiling (or directly telling her to smile more):** Would you tell Robert from accounting that he looks better when he smiles? Probably not, so avoid doing this with your female colleagues.

- **Interrupting a woman while she's speaking:** See previous section!

- Asking women with other marginalized identities (like a specific ethnicity or sexuality) to take on extra work, like DEI efforts or trainings: Instead of assuming the one LGBTQIA+

woman on your leadership team wants to put together all the programming for Pride Month at your company, step up and offer to help. Or better yet, offer a bonus for doing that work instead of expecting anyone to do it for free.

- Making assumptions about women's home lives or caregiving responsibilities: Women have to answer questions such as, "When do you plan to have children?" or "How do you balance your work with your kids' busy schedules?" more often than men. Combating this can be twofold. One, lay off asking women about motherhood or caregiving. Two, if you are genuinely curious about your colleagues' kids or their work-life balance, include men in the conversation. Maybe Joseph from HR takes off early every Monday, Wednesday, and Friday to pick up his kids because his wife is the CEO of another company and her schedule is less flexible. Sharing stories that break gender stereotypes can have a positive downstream impact.

- Saying things like "You know a lot about [subject] for a woman": Chances are, if a female colleague works at your company, she's as good at her job as you are. Discounting experience or skill level by adding the "for a woman" tag to the end of a compliment can make women feel invalidated and frustrated. And would you ever tell your male colleague, "You know a lot about engineering for a man"?

As men, we should seek ways to include women and make them feel like a valued and equal member of the organization. Here are some easy steps to take.
- Provide work-related compliments
- Consider the needs of others
- Be curious
- Build positive relationships

- Avoid assumptions
- Help other men be aware of microaggressions,
- Lead by example
- Do what's right

Can You Identify the Microaggressions in Your Workplace?

Take a look back at your professional and personal lives. Where have you seen microaggressions like these flare up? From your friends? Your colleagues? Even yourself?

The good news is it's not too late to be aware and to spread that awareness. We owe it to the women in our lives—and the ones who aren't—to not thoughtlessly victimize them. It will take men to help other men realize the impact we have on women with our words and actions. We can be better.

While awareness is the first step, it means nothing if you don't act. When you witness microaggressions—or other instances of social generational default, including gender stereotyping—speak up and defend women.

Many of us grew up with the idea that masculinity means being strong, courageous, dominating, or powerful. But now the new wave of masculinity clears space for—and even expects—men to be kind, empathetic, and sensitive. To be masculine now involves being willing to display and deal with emotions and to be champions of women in all settings.

Men can still be strong, powerful, and confident, but not at the expense of women and their position in society. And don't forget this isn't exclusive to the workplace.

Equitably Divide Responsibilities at Home

If you have a female partner at home, it's time to take an honest look at who does what and how fair that divide is. According to the Bureau of Labor Statistics, 86 percent of women spend time doing housework on an average day, compared to only 71 percent of men. Research from the Pew Research Center also indicates a big divide in the amount of time men and women spend on housework: In marriages where the wife is the primary earner, wives still did more housework (4.8 hours per week) compared to husbands (2.8 hours).

Men, meanwhile, get an extra 3.5 hours a week for their leisure activities than women do, plus three more hours a week on paid work. With women trying to climb the same career ladders as men, those extra three weekly hours add up fast.

Closing the gap starts with having an honest conversation with your partner. What are your strengths and interests when it comes to household tasks? What are hers? Is she spending more time than you on cleaning, cooking, or childcare?

Often this gap doesn't even happen intentionally. Men and women in partnerships just settle into the social generational default they've grown up with: women feel obligated to take on more of the household burden. Too often they've been told that the cleanliness and orderliness of their home is a measure of a woman's success. Men often grew up in a household where their mother lived by the same expectation. And so the cycle continues. But it doesn't have to.

Men, your role at home or within a relationship should be to be reflective, thoughtful, and inclusive. Feed off your strengths and know your weaknesses and know your partner's strengths and weaknesses. Then divide responsibilities at home to reflect those strengths.

But equity isn't just about drawing up a list of chores and splitting it down the middle. We also have to be more mindful of the "mental load" women often carry. As men we're pretty good at checking off a task and then moving on. But women often take on more of the burden of looking ahead to what needs to be done *next*. For instance, how much do you think about the number of toilet paper rolls you have in reserve? Do you think about when your child's appointments are, which vehicle needs an oil change, when to water the plants, and whose birthday is coming up? When men fail to take on some of these responsibilities, women take on the burden.

Think of it like a basketball team. It's great to be the center who's really good at dunking the ball each time he gets thrown a lob. But the mental load of that isn't as high as the point guard who's thinking ahead, reading defenses, and getting teammates into position.

It's time to take on more point-guard duties, in other words.

Here's where strengths and weaknesses come into play. If you're a good cook and thrive with grocery shopping and meal planning, you should take on more or all food-related responsibility (and yes, that means planning lists ahead of time, mapping out kids' lunches, and keeping an eye on when you're running low on garlic—not just cooking day to day). If you're better at keeping track of longer-term things like vehicle maintenance or vacation planning, take on those responsibilities.

When each partner leans into your strengths and relieve each other of weaknesses, more headspace will be cleared for spontaneous activities which will ultimately help you build and maintain a better relationship while also avoiding resentment and strain.

Melissa, thanks for loaning me the mic briefly. You take it from here.

"Be skinny. Have a family."

ALIGN

<u>A</u>waken to the Default

<u>L</u>isten to Your Inner Compass

<u>I</u>nterrupt the Pattern

<u>G</u>ive Yourself Permission

<u>N</u>avigate with Intention

CHAPTER 5

Awaken to the Default

Now that you understand the social generational default—what it is, how it shows up, and what our responsibilities and limitations are to replace it—it's time to learn the ALIGN framework for how to navigate this default in your own life and career.

This four-step process is one I've spent decades developing after working with hundreds of women, both alongside them in the corporate world or as their coach. Instead of using a variety of examples to illustrate how to move through these steps, we'll use *one person's* story.

Starting in this chapter, you'll follow the evolution of Lina as she moves through the four steps. Every challenge, every conversation, and and every win from this composite story is based on a real-world situation with a woman I've personally known or coached.

Lina was a marine systems engineer on the East Coast who oversaw the repair of internal systems of marine vessels. In her role, she led a team of twelve maintenance professionals—all men.

Despite being the only woman in her position and not having any women in positions above hers, Lina wanted to eventually be promoted to marine project engineer (MPE) within her yard. At the time she was thirty-seven years old with a PhD, and she believed it was time to move up. Within the MPE role, she would oversee her own team of junior engineers, take charge of the budget, and be the liaison between her team and the overall project supervisor.

But a lot stood in the way of her reaching that goal.

Like many other women in male-dominated industries, Lina dealt with near-constant microaggressions. Her colleagues frequently dismissed her comments, challenged her solutions, and even took credit for her ideas. She was interrupted in meetings. Little "compliments" from her colleagues just felt like masked insults: "It's impressive you've made it this far. Most women drop out." Or "For a woman, you really know your stuff!"

All of this felt like a relic from a previous era. But it was the 2020s, and Lina was frustrated with all the default stereotypes she couldn't seem to escape. And it wasn't just at work where Lina dealt with these gender stereotypes. She heard pieces of it from her family, too.

"Why do you need to work like this?" Lina's mom frequently asked. "The kids need you. Daycare and their teachers can't raise them. Look at the job Marc has—you shouldn't even have to work!"

It was true: Lina's husband, Marc, had an excellent job as the CFO of a national advertising agency. But Lina couldn't help but wonder: *Why isn't anyone telling Marc that he shouldn't work so hard and he should stay home with the kids more? Nobody is encouraging him to tamper his ambition.* Internalizing this gendered messaging from society and family is the **social generational default**. We ingest—and regurgitate—these messages without even realizing it.

Still, even when Lina *did* recognize that some of this messaging was the social generational default, she felt the pressure to be a "better" mother. Her four kids were seven, nine, eleven, and fifteen. She constantly felt guilty for missing so much of their lives. As Lina worked extra hours, Maya took her first steps. When Lina traveled to London for a conference, she missed Sophia's school play. Lina even felt guilty for not being there for homework time in the evenings. This is the power of the social generational default: It even creates guilt about things we think we're supposed to be doing or that we're supposed to be doing *better*. But we never pause long enough to evaluate these expectations from our own lenses.

On top of all this, Lina took on the bulk of housework. When she came home from an eleven-hour workday, there were always dishes in the sink—even on days when Marc beat her home and he was hours into his weeknight routine of binge-watching *Game of Thrones*. Meanwhile everything was a mess and at least one of the kids wanted dinner.

To put it lightly, Lina was exhausted. She felt stuck in her career and felt like she was a bad mom. She was tired of feeling like she could never do or be "enough." She was tired of hearing from everyone else about why she wasn't enough. And there was a constant, loud voice inside her head that spent good chunks of each day parroting pieces of the social generational default back to her: *You're so lazy for not going on that run this morning! Why are you aiming for that promotion? You don't have nearly enough expertise.*

No matter how hard Lina worked, it felt like there was an invisible barrier between where she was and who she dreamed of becoming.

Action #1: Take Stock of What's *Not Working* in Your Current Reality

To move outside the social generational default and craft a new, more aligned reality for yourself and future generations, you have to understand your starting point. You can't know where you're going until you recognize where you are. What's making you miserable? What about your life and career isn't working? What is working? What are the things you feel you're expected to do that you don't even like or believe in?

For Lina, her "not working" list looked like this.

- Her colleagues' microaggressions
- The messages from her grandmother that she always needed to be "pretty and put together"
- The painfully slow—if not outright stalled—promotional track she seemed to be on
- Her mother's well-meaning, but ultimately unhelpful, comments about how much Lina was working instead of staying at home

- Her own sense of "mom guilt"
- Marc's lack of support with the housework

Meanwhile, her "what *is* working" list included these things.
- The *actual* work she did: she loved a systematic, logical approach to solving problems and dealing with the inner workings of the vessel
- Her parents lived nearby and were available to help with the kids when needed
- She loved where she lived and her work commute was short
- She was grateful that—unlike some of her other female friends in the corporate world—she didn't ever feel pressure to wear heels or a skirt to work

Action #2: Identify Your Messaging

Not everything that feels like a struggle in your life or career will fall back onto the social generational default. The economy might still suck. Your kids will still get sick. Life will have its busy seasons, and everyone gets stressed.

But many of the things keeping women back can relate back to the messaging that society throws on us all.

So it's time to get intimately familiar with your internal messaging: What those messages are, where they come from, and if they *actually reflect* who and what you want to be at your core. Sometimes the answer will be yes; sometimes it'll be no. What's important is that you consistently ask yourself those questions.

For Lina, this meant taking into account all the ways in which she ingested society's expectations: TV advertisements, magazines, social media, her parents, her husband, and her coworkers.

Lina remembered watching her mother take on all the household and parenting responsibilities and retire early from her nursing career. Lina's dad came home from work, sat down to a prepared dinner, and then spent the evening on the couch while her mom cleaned up. Even today, her father *still* didn't know where to put the clean dishes if he took them out of the dishwasher.

How much of that had Lina internalized? Is that where her "mom guilt" came from?

Meanwhile Lina thought back to all the messaging she received in school about her intelligence and knack for engineering and math. Every compliment seemed to be punctuated with "for a girl" at the end. Then there were the not-so-subtle "this isn't your place" comments, like when Lina asked to be put into AP calculus, and the school counselor responded with, "Wouldn't you be more comfortable in AP English?" Had Lina somehow internalized that she didn't belong in this industry because it was constantly pointed out that her talent was "unusual"?

Action #3: Integrate a Pause

Unwinding the messaging that's been ingrained into your brain can be a long process—years if not a whole lifetime. You likely learned from an early age that you need to avoid conflict, be "nice," or accommodate everyone's needs but your own. Recognizing and rewriting that message is a process you'll have to engage with daily.

One small step you can take in the day-to-day in order to start recording over some of that messaging is to *pause*.

In a situation where you can feel yourself start to slip into default mode—doing what you feel like you "should" do or prioritizing being "nice" over saying what you actually mean to a demanding colleague—take a deep breath. Count to ten in your head. Clear some brain space and really think about how you want to respond.

The first time Lina tried this was when one of her male colleagues asked her a question she was *certain* he wouldn't have asked his fellow male coworkers. At the conclusion of an important meeting—which Lina led—Jerry asked, "You've done a great job with the team so far. Do you think you'll be able to stay in this role after you have more kids?" Her default reaction would have been to brush off the assumption and move on. As the only woman in her department, she didn't want to be labeled difficult or too sensitive. But instead of falling back into that rut, she took a beat and decided to respond more consciously.

In the moment, ten seconds can feel like an *eternity*. You'll want to fill the silence. You'll want to burrow into the floor to escape the discomfort. But those ten seconds are also the least you can offer yourself to take a miniature break, evaluate the situation, identify your habitual response, and choose a more intentional, aligned path.

Instead of smiling away the assumptions Jerry had made—both that Lina *would* have more kids and that her role as a mother would interfere with her work—Lina paused.

Then she said, "Listen, Jerry, I really value open communication and our professional relationship, so I'm going to give you some feedback. That kind of comment is both sexist and intrusive. My husband and I may or may not choose to have more kids. Whatever we end up deciding, that won't impact my ability to do my job. Plus, would you ask Keenan the same question about his role?"

Often men make these kinds of comments and assumptions without realizing it's insulting or inappropriate. This is where pausing and giving that gift of feedback is so important. Jerry might feel bad for assuming and adjust his behavior next time.

That said, it's also important not to expect any particular outcome. Calling out microaggressions and communicating openly is often the right thing to do regardless—*even if and when* the recipient doesn't listen or change their behavior. At least you'll know internally you did everything you could and are living by your personal values.

This "pause" strategy can apply in a digital setting too. Maybe you receive an email from a male coworker asking you to take on a low-level task that an intern could probably handle. Out of habit, you might default to saying "yes" because you don't want to be "difficult" or seem uncooperative. But instead of falling back into that same pattern, click away from the email, close your eyes, and breathe in. Count to ten. Check in with yourself. Do you actually *want* to take on the extra responsibility? Are you truly the only qualified person to take it on? Can you ask for extra resources or support from colleagues to get it done? Will taking on that responsibility take you away from your actual job duties? What does your gut tell you about saying yes? How does it feel when you think about saying no?

Even if you don't make a final decision about what to do in those ten seconds, you can use that pause to buy yourself more time. Stop yourself from the obligatory "yes" and instead say, "I need to think about this a little more. Let me get back to you with an answer by the end of this week."

Remember: it's okay to ask for more time. You don't always have to deliver a "yes" in the moment. You don't even have to deliver one at all. The point is to take the time you need to arrive at a conclusion that feels right for *you*.

Bonus tip and template: Just because the conversation is over doesn't mean it's *done*. If you've responded in a habitual way that doesn't align with your goals or values, it's okay to revisit the topic and change your mind later. Here's a sample script for when you might need to reignite a conversation.

"Hi [insert boss name], I know I previously said yes to showing the new hires around the office. But after taking another look at my workload, I don't have the bandwidth. Is there a way to pull in an additional person from the team to help out? I've also made a list (see below) of some low-priority items on my plate that we can potentially push to next quarter. Let me know if I should clear some time that way! If you want to discuss further, I'm happy to connect for a quick call."

Break the Script Exercise #1: Identify Your Default Messaging

Before you can rewire your life, make different choices, and fight back against conformity, you have to recognize where that default is showing up for you.

Use the prompts below as starting points to identify all the messages, expectations, or beliefs you've received from your family, friends, community, partner, or the media.

1. What messages about how to be a woman did your family raise you with?
2. What are the messages you received from society about how to be a woman?
3. Finish this sentence: "As a woman, I'm supposed to be/do _____."

It also might be beneficial to break this down into different buckets For example, write down the messages you've received about the following.

- What your responsibilities are
- What makes you successful or unsuccessful
- What "desirable" traits are
- How to get promoted
- What you want other people to say about you
- How to deal with conflict and disagreement
- Women's leadership qualities

If you want to dive into the social generational default in other, nonwork aspects of your life, here are a few ideas.
- Body image and health
- The choice of whether or not to have kids

- How to be a good partner/spouse
- How to dress and/or present yourself (in the workplace and outside of it)

Remember that it can take some time to fully recognize these defaults. Unconscious conformity to societal and generational expectations—especially as women—happens insidiously. That's what makes it unconscious, after all. Take your time. And be kind to yourself. Conforming to societal expectations hammered into you for years or decades is *not* a character flaw. Some of these default settings may have even benefited you throughout your life! All of that is okay. The point of this exercise is to note everything and start evaluating which of these expectations or beliefs match your core values and goals.

Saying "no" to a societal expectation and choosing a different path doesn't come without risk. Later in this book, we'll dive into potential consequences of these changes in behavior.

But *conformity* comes with its own level of risk too. The next chapter is about how the social generational default may undermine women's happiness, self-esteem, confidence, and more, both personally and professionally. In fact, it may be one of the things keeping the patriarchy humming.

CHAPTER 6

Listen to Your Inner Compass

How many times have you pulled into a parking space at your destination only to realize you can't even remember making the specific turns to get there? You were on autopilot the whole time and the world just flew by out your window. Muscle memory took over and defaulted to familiar highway on-ramps. You didn't even have to think about it.

Too often this is how we move through life: on autopilot down the well-worn track of social generational default.

A few years into her career, Lina realized that's exactly what had happened to her. She was growing increasingly frustrated with her colleagues' microaggressions, her seeming lack of upward mobility at her organization, and the crippling burnout she felt.

Lina had been so wrapped up in the day-to-day, so underwater with her to-do list, so overwhelmed at work and home, that she had never stopped to consider whether she was living by the core values she actually identified with rather than those she had been conditioned to have since birth.

On second thought, she hadn't paused to think about what those values even *were*. She woke up to the blare of her alarm in the predawn hours and rushed into her day like a sprinter coming off the starting blocks. That unsustainable pace was overwhelming, of course. But she also felt disconnected from her own life. She was tired of seeking approval from others, being afraid of others' judgment, and feeling like she was handing her power over to a default expectation she never explicitly agreed to. Sometimes it felt like she wasn't blazing her own path, she was instead running someone else's race.

But Lina was ready to change course and live by *her* values—not the ones placed upon her by society.

Her first step was hiring an executive coach. Lina was wise enough to grasp that she didn't know what she didn't know. Plus she wanted a fresh perspective from someone who wasn't related to her and didn't work with her. Sometimes you're just too close to your own life (*as you should be!*), and it's hard to zoom out to the thirty-thousand-foot view to objectively evaluate what's going on.

This is the crux of why so many people fall into the social generational default without realizing it. Many of us don't know what our core values are, so many of us can't tell when we're off track from them.

With a little extra intention, you can opt out and head down a different path. Maybe there's no "right" or "wrong" path, but there is *your chosen path*. Your core values will help map that out.

Lina and I sat down with a whiteboard on which I wrote fifty words. The goal was to start broad with a wide variety of concepts, then narrow in on the ones that spoke to Lina's soul. On the board, there was everything from *morality* and *cooperation* to *trustworthiness* and *loyalty*.

When she first looked at the list, Lina felt a little overwhelmed. "Of course I believe in integrity and personal growth. But do they really drive *me* at my core?!"

These are all big questions, and it can help to spend some time with them. The answers won't always pop out immediately. Try to give yourself the space and time to dig deep. What makes you who you are? What values or concepts trigger feelings of unsettledness, stress, or disappointment when someone in your life doesn't follow them?

You'll also find an exercise at the end of this chapter to choose your own personal values. But first, here's what Lina decided.

Balance: Lina cringed a little at the phrase "work-life balance." ("That shit just doesn't exist!" she told me.) She couldn't help but feel like it was an unattainable pie in the sky. And in some ways, she's right. But she still felt at her core that she needed more balance in her life, whatever that would end up looking like. She needed to fill her cup more often, rather than constantly pouring out her last few drops for everyone else. She couldn't keep putting in twelve-hour days, then coming home and spending her few precious "leisure" hours making sure the household actually ran properly. Sure, this meant washing the sink full of dirty dishes or vacuuming the crumbs from the living room carpet. But Lina found herself also taking on the high-level planning responsibilities of their life—knowing when to order more dog food, realizing Marc's mom's birthday was that upcoming weekend and making plans for dinner, or making sure the property taxes got paid on time. If she didn't do these things, too often they just didn't get done. Even beyond her work schedule, which was overstuffed, Lina felt a fundamental imbalance between her and her husband. Why couldn't he just *occasionally* take on vacation planning or buy his mother a birthday card? Why did it feel like she didn't have a true *partner* working alongside her in her life? He would do whatever she asked, and her friends loved to tell her how "lucky" she was that he was so "helpful." But she didn't want to have to ask. Completing the tasks was the easy part. She needed help with *proactive* household management.

Openness: Whether it was in a conversation with a friend or discussing a problem with a colleague, Lina appreciated transparency. She hated feeling like she couldn't talk about certain things with the people in her life or like she couldn't directly confront uncomfortable realities. In her daily work life, she felt a lot of uncomfortable friction because the organization's culture rewarded what she saw as a black-box mentality. Employees who were often late or who exhibited bad performance were allowed to stay on board, or even promoted. But there was little transparency or open communication about why. When people asked questions, the bosses made them feel like troublemakers or they were simply ignored. Lina realized this was one of the biggest problems she had with her current job because it grated up against who she was as a person. She was direct and honest. And she was realizing that any other way of being was creating extreme levels of stress and discomfort.

Authenticity: Lina preferred minimal makeup, a low-maintenance hairstyle, and she was comfortable with who she was. She didn't want to squeeze into some arbitrary idea of "professionalism," especially in an industry with so few women and when the definition in her sector had been written almost exclusively by men. Lina hated playing that game and just wanted to *herself.* As long as she got the job done, who cared whether she wore a pantsuit? Who cared whether she was a touch "too assertive"?

Quick Tips for Picking Personal Values

- **Less is sometimes more.** Having only one core value probably doesn't encompass all the layers of life. But choosing ten of them can take away focus. Pick three that really resonate: that's the sweet spot.
- **Try to write the definition of "value" words that speak to you.** If they sound nice (or like what you "should" choose), but you can't actually define them, that might not be your value! *And that's okay.*

> • **Separate values you were raised with and values that resonate with you now as an adult.** This can be valuable because it helps you recognize ways you've evolved and ways you've remained the same.

After nailing down three of her core values, Lina knew she still had a long way to go. Just identifying a few words wasn't going to change her workplace culture or her marriage.

But to choose a new route for your life and career, you have to cultivate a sense of direction. Think of your core values as your internal GPS—so the next time you get behind the wheel and your brain slides into autopilot, you'll know *you* intentionally programmed it. Let's rewrite those factory settings.

Break the Script Exercise #2: Choose Your Own Core Values

Browse through this list of potential personal core values. Circle the seven (7) that speak the most to you.

Acceptance	*Citizenship*
Achievement	*Commitment*
Accountability	*Community*
Action	*Compassion*
Adventure	*Competency*
Authority	*Confidence*
Autonomy	*Contribution*
Authenticity	*Conviction*
Balance	*Courage*
Beauty	*Curiosity*
Boldness	*Creativity*
Challenge	*Determination*

Empathy

Excellence

Fairness Growth

Faith

Fame

Friendship

Frugality

Fun

Generosity

Grace

Happiness

Harmony

Honesty

Humor

Imagination

Independence

Individuality

Integrity

Influence

Joy

Justice

Kindness

Knowledge

Leadership

Learning

Logic

Love

Loyalty

Meaning

Modesty

Openness

Optimism

Organization

Originality

Patience

Peace

Perseverance

Poise

Popularity

Recognition

Reputation

Resilience

Respect

Responsibility

Security

Self-awareness

Self-reliance

Self-respect

Service

Simplicity

Sincerity

Spirituality

Stability

Status

Strength

Success

Trustworthiness

Wealth

Wisdom

Then do the following three steps.
1. Make a list of your top seven values from the list above (or include words of your own!).
2. From the list of seven, cross out two.
3. From the list of five, cross out two more. What values does that leave? Are they the ones you absolutely don't want to live without? Which ones feel the closest to your personality, your deepest desires, and your goals?

Follow-up Questions: To help you understand whether your life and work are aligned with your personal core values, journal about these questions:

- Do I feel a sense of fulfillment and purpose in what I do, or do I constantly make compromises that leave me feeling disconnected from my true self?
- When making decisions—big or small—do I prioritize what truly matters to me, or do I find myself following societal, familial, or workplace expectations instead?
- If I removed external pressures (money, opinions, tradition), would I still choose the same career, relationships, and daily habits that I have now?

CHAPTER 7

Interrupt the Pattern and Give Yourself Permission

It's tempting to fall into the belief that moving forward in your career or living a happier life is all about what you say "yes" to: that extra opportunity that will lead to promotion, the longer hours to impress your boss, the after-hours email responses so you can appear "committed."

But research shows that people who say "no" more often are happier, more satisfied, and more connected to their personal values. Saying "yes" too often can lead to stress, being overwhelmed, and exhaustion. (But you probably already knew this.)

What you might not know is this: According to research from Baylor's Katharine O'Brien, social norms play a major role in women being more likely than men to say "yes" to extra work. According to O'Brien, "Women typically are regarded as nurturers and helpers, so saying 'no' runs against the grain of what might be expected of them." Often women also end up having these expectations of *ourselves*—it's how most of us were raised.

In your own life, it's probably easy to come up with a long list of women you personally know who are overworked, stretched too thin, and rarely say "no" when asked to add more. It's a lot harder to think of women we know who rarely say "yes."

As author Anne Lamott popularized: "'No' is a complete sentence."

Saying "no" more often is one of the simplest—and most radical—

ways to step outside of the social generational default. And crucially, saying "no" to the situations or people who don't help us live by our values opens up space to say "yes" to the ones who will.

This is a lesson Lina knew she had to put into practice. But in the gap between Lina's current life and the one she wanted, she knew there needed to be a lot more "no"—or at least some "not right now." So we worked together to figure out where her day-to-day didn't match her values and which of those gaps she would no longer tolerate. It was also important to recognize where she was willing to bend a little. Values aren't rigid structures that bind us to a certain way of living. They can flex with our lives, desires, and schedules.

So one day, Lina let Marc know that he needed to take care of the kids while she headed to her go-to coffee shop for a couple hours. She sat down with a latte, a pen, and paper to brainstorm how she wasn't living according to her values and what she needed to start saying "no" to. Below is the chart is the chart Lina came up with. There's also a blank one at the end of this chapter you can use for yourself.

Value	What I'm okay with continuing	What I won't tolerate anymore
Balance	• Some housework, as long as Marc takes on an equal share. We need to divide up the tasks and figure out a minimum acceptable standard. • Also okay with lowering some standards and letting go of the need for perfection!	• Working on nights and weekends. • Not enough time to spend with family. • Always saying "yes" to the new direct report when she asks for help after-hours when I know she's perfectly capable of figuring out solutions on her own.

Value	What I'm okay with continuing	What I won't tolerate anymore
Authenticity	• Wearing a business suit to appear professional, even if I don't love the company's idea of "business casual."	• Having to wear a full face of makeup or keep a high-maintenance hairstyle. No man is held to these standards, so I'm not going to force myself into that box either!
Openness	• When someone questions my ideas *but* is open and honest about their reasoning and is genuinely curious without being confrontational or dismissive.	• Staying quiet about microaggressions at work. When coworkers say things like "You're pretty tough for a woman" or call me "honey," I want to be open with them about why this isn't okay. • My team is going over my head to report that I'm "too demanding." We need to be able to openly discuss expectations, management style, or communication preferences without pulling in the (male) bosses.

Value	What I'm okay with continuing	What I won't tolerate anymore
Openness cont'd		• Being afraid of openness. I'm not going to stop myself from asking for help or expressing concerns anymore just because I'm scared I'll be perceived as weak or lacking self-confidence.

Sticking to Your Values and Defying the "Likability Bias"

Saying "no," of course, isn't as easy as we'd like it to be. As O'Brien's research found, women are seen as the "nurturers" and "helpers." So when you step outside of that mold, the backlash can be strong. One major hurdle you'll likely experience is "likability bias."

"Likability bias" describes the tendency to view powerful, successful women less favorably because they challenge societal expectations of female kindness and accommodation. The more powerful they become, the less "nice" they seem, especially to those who have internalized societal stereotypes about gender dynamics. The more that powerful women speak up, call out inequity, and fight for change, the more they fall down the "nice"—and therefore likability—scale.

Take pop star Taylor Swift, for example. When she first came onto the music scene, she was seen as largely unobjectionable—a nice girl with a guitar. As her star power rose—and her bank account, as she eventually crossed the billionaire threshold—so did people's attacks on her. They said she wrote too much about her ex-boyfriends (aka, she wasn't nice enough to them). When she danced in the audience at awards shows, people claimed she was attention-starved or "too much." When she began dating NFL star Travis Kelce, football fans claimed it ruined games when camera crews showed her too much on TV broadcasts. The 2025 Super Bowl audience even booed her on the stadium's jumbotron.

There are countless other examples. WNBA and former Iowa women's basketball star Caitlin Clark is labeled too passionate or too aggressive. Meghan, Duchess of Sussex (née Markle) is viewed as power hungry or controlling. Beyoncé is seen as too loud or overt about her experiences as a Black woman in the US. Hillary Rodham Clinton is conveyed as too calculated or cold. This list could carry on endlessly.

These are all powerful, successful women who have faced the "unlikeable" moniker, either because of the power they've attained, the fact they don't fit into the "nice lady" mold society expects of them, or because they rocked the boat and stood up for what they believe.

While you may not be a billionaire, a duchess, or an elite athlete (yet!), you still have power. With every inch of success you attain and every step you take closer to living by your most core values, you may have to fight against a corresponding loss of "likability."

How and When to Pick Your Battles

If you had a dollar for every time someone gave you the advice to "pick your battles," you could probably buy yourself a pretty nice dinner. But *how* do you know how to choose? How do you decide whether something goes against your core principles? What's worth pursuing? What's better letting go? When does the potential benefit of speaking up or saying "no" outweigh the risk of being "unlikable" or difficult?

Those dividing lines are different for everyone. Here are a few questions to ask yourself to gauge whether something that's internally nagging at you is worth challenging in your workplace.

- What is at stake?
- Do you have an ally in the situation? Is there someone who will go to battle alongside you?

- Would the overall organizational culture be supportive?
- Is there an opportunity to educate someone? (For example, an older male coworker consistently comments on your clothing at the office. Would it be valuable to let him know this is inappropriate towards women in the workplace before you try to take the issue to HR?)

Break the Script Exercise #3: Decide What It's Time to Stop and What's Okay to Continue

Think back to the three core values you chose in Chapter 6. Are there aspects of your life that fly in the face of those principles? Are there aspects that could continue that wouldn't drastically upset your values? You can use the chart below to take notes or just pique your curiosity.

Value	What I'm okay with continuing	What I won't tolerate anymore

CHAPTER 8

<u>N</u>avigate with Intention

Imagine you're on a crowded beach, craning your neck over hordes of people to get a glimpse of the ocean. And forget swimming: you can't even get close to the water. The space is so packed that people keep shoving you backward when you try to take a step forward.

As you peek over someone's shoulder, you see a small island in the distance. You can tell from the long strips of white sand that it's much less crowded and much more peaceful. It seems like a way better beach on which to spend your time. Now you just need a boat to get yourself from point A to point B.

This chapter is about how to build your boat—in other words, how to move from your current reality to a more peaceful, truer-to-you life. In Chapter 7, you decided what is acceptable—*and unacceptable*—about your current situation. Now you'll develop a plan to shed the unacceptable parts, improve the acceptable ones, and connect your day-to-day life with your core values.

But none of us live in a utopia. There are real risks to bucking society's expectations for women. There are formidable systemic hurdles standing in our way when we do choose a different path. So before crafting any plan or changing any behaviors, you'll need to clarify what you're up against. Armed with that information, you'll be able to make the most educated, confident choice about what to do next.

Understand the Systemic Hurdles Standing in the Way of Conscious Choice

Each of our paths is influenced by other people, no matter how independent we want to be. Bosses, coworkers, parents, friends, children, partners, siblings, neighbors, and even that person driving only twenty miles an hour in front of you all sometimes have an impact on our day-to-day—and our ability to make certain choices.

Zooming out to the macro level, we also live within a society that still has systemic sexism, racism, and other prejudices baked in. Individual shifts in behavior can do only so much when we're faced with poor parental leave policies, eroding workplace protections, a lack of generational wealth, or other systemic barriers, such as the gender pay gap.

For example, you may be ready to pursue that next promotion. But then your mom gets sick, and she's already drained most of her retirement savings on treatment. Because of the lack of affordable elder care, you have to either shell out huge sums of money to fill the gaps or take on caregiving duties yourself. Suddenly those longer hours don't seem so viable.

Maybe you're a parent who wants to take on a higher-level management position after having your first child. But when you can't find affordable child care, and your partner has no access to paid parental leave, taking on a new opportunity isn't so easy.

Or maybe you're someone like Lina, facing down the systemic sexism within a male-dominated field like engineering.

No one person can solve big systemic issues. But what we *can* do is recognize our unique circumstances, take stock of the system in which those circumstances exist, do what we can with what we have, and continue to work together with other women and allies to change the system for the better for future generations.

Understand the Risks of Resisting the Social Generational Default

When you step outside of any prescribed path, there will be some turbulence. However, assessing risk and recognizing some of the issues that can pop up will help you stay ahead of potential consequences. When you move toward conscious choice and away from the social generational default, you might experience some challenges.

- **Potential backlash or retaliation:** To put it lightly, not everyone will be thrilled when you step outside the default expectations for women and start playing by your own rules. You could be labeled a problem or you could even be passed over for a promotion in the future. Everyone's situation is unique, so it's important to do a thorough risk assessment of your workplace dynamics before making behavior shifts.

- **Get sucked into the double bind:** One major risk of conscious choice is pretty much *never* being able to win. If you speak up for yourself and fight against gender stereotypes, you could be labeled "hard to get along with" or "difficult." But on the other hand, if you stay in the "likable" lane, you may not garner the same respect as male colleagues. It's very difficult for women to find the right balance between warmth and power. Falling too far to one end of the spectrum will be a risk for as long as the social generational default exists for women.

- **Add to your workload:** For some there might be comfort attached to abiding by the social generational default. When you start carving your own path, the uphill climb can feel steep. You might have to take on more responsibility, have more difficult conversations, or make really hard choices. All of this can add to your workload, especially in the short term.

Even within this reality, there are some ways to mitigate or deal with these risks.

- **Build a community at work:** Most women feel alone when they experience sexism or other gender-based stereotyping. Validation of your experiences and finding support to reduce isolation are enormously important. When you have others to lean on in the workplace, everything else gets easier. Foster relationships with other women you work with, and don't forget about male allies too. Both can provide value or support when you have a tough conversation with your boss, are passed over for promotion, or need advice. Plus, the stronger your community, the easier it will be to find folks to celebrate with when you do hit your goals!

- **Ask for concrete feedback from your boss:** Research has shown that women often receive vaguer feedback than their male colleagues at work—and it's often related more to emotions or relationships rather than business results. When you have check-in meetings with your boss, make sure they're giving you actionable, results-oriented feedback. If you're worried about potential retaliation for bringing up a long-standing issue to your boss, such as asking for more money or trying to get the next promotion, try to arm yourself with as many hard facts and data points as you can. Connect your accomplishments back to business results, and pull whatever numbers can help you prove that impact: sales percentages, turnover rates for your team, project timelines, etc.

- **Let go of expectations of a certain outcome or behavior change:** Moving away from the social generational default and operating with more conscious choices is not about attaining specific outcomes. It's a mindset by which you design your life, a framework to make decisions, and a call for you to take ownership over what you can control in your life and career. The more you can focus on that journey rather than specific end results (salary, title, award, or behavior change, for example), the more supportive this structure can be. The important thing is that you make these conscious choices because they're the right choices *for you*. These choices are aligned with your values, even if they don't always have control over the end results.

- **Remember who and what you're fighting for:** The risks of facing down the social generational default and challenging gender stereotypes can be big. They can feel scary. But it's also important to understand the risks of *not* challenging these stereotypes where and when we can. Think of a specific stereotype or expectation of women that you want to speak up about. Is it something you would want your own daughter, niece, or younger colleague to face in her own career? If not, then the risk of standing up against that expectation might be worth the long-term benefit, even if you don't see those direct benefits in your *own* career.

Build Your Action Plan to Push Your Reality Closer to Your Core Values

Once you get a handle on your circumstances and any systemic barriers or risks you need to circumnavigate, you'll want to revisit that list of core values you drew up in Chapter 6. Taking into account your individual challenges and circumstances, what action steps can you take to connect your current reality back to those values? What bridges can you build?

It helps to break your action steps down into buckets. Evaluate each value individually and build an action plan for each.

For Lina's core values—balance, authenticity, and openness—it looked like this.

Balance: Chuck the Mindset of Being "Everything to Everyone" Out the Window

One of Lina's first steps was calling BS on the idea of "having it all." She didn't want it all. She certainly didn't want to carry the load of running a household if she was also taking on all the responsibilities at her job. "All" felt like a trap set by . . . yep, the social generational default. Take on more than you can bear, and don't you dare complain or be difficult!

When we have a mindset that we want it all, we end up putting ourselves last. We try to be everything to everyone—and we leave our own needs in the dust.

For Lina, letting go of this mindset felt like a four-hundred-pound gorilla off her back. She started daydreaming about *all* the things she could let go of: the idea that her house had to be Instagram-clean all the time, the belief that she had to put in eleven-hour workdays to get ahead, or the obligation she felt to powerlift at 5 a.m. If a little cellulite came along with her as she climbed the ladder in her industry, she decided that was okay.

She also decided to stop answering emails after 8 p.m., and she directly communicated that boundary with her team. Even when her direct reports reached out with questions or problems, Lina encouraged them to work through it themselves until she was back in the office the next day. By doing this, she not only cut down her own working hours, but she also set an example for the next generation that it was okay to shut down the email app after dinner.

Authenticity: Using Natural Assertiveness as a Strength

By her nature, Lina was an assertive person. But she'd been watering down that trait at work. She was exhausted with buttering herself up just to sound "nicer" or more "approachable." Worrying so much about how people were going to perceive her had even begun to chip away at her self-confidence. She wanted to reconnect with the belief that she was good at her job and was a strong leader.

Lina certainly wasn't *mean*, and directness was her strong suit. Somewhere along the way in her career, she'd let that characteristic fall to the wayside. It wasn't lost on her that an assertive male in her position would likely be lauded for his "strong leadership."

But once she connected with authenticity as one of her core values and recognized that she wasn't being her true, authentic self at work, Lina knew she wanted to get back to her natural directness. A conversation with her boss was warranted, she decided. She would go to him and explain that her leadership style wasn't rude or "too much"—it drove results. In fact, she found a term for this kind of leadership during her research: "compassionate candor"—aka being both kind and direct. This type of leadership actually drives higher team performance, productivity, employee retention, and faster decision-making.

Openness: Have the Tough Conversations, Build Trust

Lina decided she was going to be more open about calling out the microaggressions she experienced at work—and would do so thoughtfully. For example, the sixty-four-year-old who was just a few months short of retirement who constantly called her "honey"? Maybe that wasn't worth the time or effort to call out.

But with other guys on her team who joked about how she could take a joke pretty well "for a woman," or she was tough "for a woman," or anything else "for a woman" . . . well, it was time to face those comments directly. She decided to directly talk with her team. She would lead with clarity and kindness, not anger or defensiveness.

She also wanted to work to reestablish trust and create a culture of psychological safety and openness so they would come to her with issues instead of talking to others or going above her head. To do this, she took the following action steps.

1. Modeled vulnerability herself. Lina chose to be open about mistakes or areas where she was still learning and developing.
2. Actively invited input from the whole team. If someone was

on the quieter side, she made an extra effort to solicit their feedback, even if they didn't volunteer it at first.

3. Responded to team members' mistakes with curiosity rather than judgment.

Exercise #4—Write Your New Script: Navigate with Intention

You've read how life can look radically different when we choose to live by conscious choice instead of the social generational default. Now it's your turn to apply that shift and create an action plan in your own life.

Step 1: Spot the Default

Choose one area of your life that we explored in Chapter 3.

- ☐ Autonomy & values
- ☐ Gender stereotypes
- ☐ Balance at home
- ☐ Professional network & mentorship
- ☐ Negotiation & salary

Take a deep breath. Now ask yourself: Where am I operating on autopilot in this area? Whose expectations am I following—are they actually mine?

Step 2: Imagine the Conscious Choice Version of Your Life

Now imagine: If no one else's expectations mattered, what would *you* choose? Don't hold back—give yourself permission to dream without editing.

If this part of my life reflected my own values, it would look like . . .

Step 3: Your First Tiny Step

What's *one small thing* you can do this week to move away from the default and toward the life you just envisioned?

Pro tip: Tiny changes compound. Don't wait for a perfect moment. Start now with what you have.

Bonus: What You Gain

Every conscious shift isn't about what you lose—it's about what you *gain*.

What's one thing you'll gain by making this shift? (Energy? Time? Confidence? Peace?)

You've just taken your first step toward designing a life that's fully yours. Welcome to living *unscripted*.

Rinse, Repeat

Repeat this exercise for as many slices of your life as you want. You can use the list above that we moved through in Chapter 3, or you can add your own.

"There are not
as many women
leaders because
they're not
as ambitious
as men."

Epilogue

There's an old riddle that goes something like this: A man and his son are in a bad car accident and are both rushed to the hospital. It turns out that the young boy needs surgery. But then the surgeon says, "I can't operate on him. He's my son." How is this possible?

The answer, of course, is that the surgeon is a woman—the boy's mother.

The fact that this is even a "riddle" where the answer isn't obvious to everyone says a lot about the expectations we have for men and women. If we fall into the rut of the social generational default, we assume doctors are men. Women are nurses. Men are the lawyers while women are the paralegals.

When my client Alexa, who has a PhD in chemistry, was brought on stage to speak at a prestigious conference, she was introduced by only her first and last name after hearing every male presenter introduced with "doctor" in front of their names.

Not every single person believes in gendered expectations. But the social generational default is the default for a reason: It shows up enough to form a pattern. That pattern warrants reconsideration and a rewrite. That's exactly what this book is for: to help you recognize those default patterns, carefully evaluate which of those expectations you *do* want to follow, and craft a more authentic plan for the slices of life in which you *don't* want to follow the default.

For now, the social generational default is still all around us. Female leaders are still seen as "aggressive" or "demanding," whereas male leaders with the same traits are "strong" or "inspirational." Women are still expected not to make a "big deal" out of microaggressions or outright sexism. There are still work cultures in which men are allowed to openly feminize and sexualize a piece of work equipment, like a robot. Women still take on the mental load of managing a household. For women who choose to have kids, "mom guilt" and all the impossible expectations we have for mothers are layered on top.

Some of these instances of the social generational default may seem tiny. Others might feel massive and insurmountable. Rewriting our own script as women is not an overnight process. It's a *lifetime* process filled with consistent action, evaluation, and experimentation.

The script you want to follow in your life and career will also likely change as your values and priorities change. Industries evolve. Elderly parents get sick. You move cities. You have a baby, or decide that you won't have a baby. In short, life happens. And as it does, the path you want to pursue professionally and personally will likely shapeshift too. When you feel confident about your core values and empowered with the strategies to pursue more conscious choice in your life, you'll be able to stick closer to your authentic path, whatever that looks like.

As a collective, this work is as important as ever. When women can lead more authentic, values-driven lives, and when they're empowered to climb career ladders in male-dominated industries, we all benefit. Companies with leadership made up of at least 30 percent women are 12 times more likely to be top performers financially. When businesses avoid losing women in leadership, they also avoid an expensive turnover problem. According to Gallup, the work to replace someone in a leadership or management position costs roughly double whatever their salary was.

Feminism has pushed women forward and made progress with issues of equality and equity. But there is still a long way to go. That's especially true for women who have historically been left out of previous waves of feminism (women of color, those in the LGBTQIA+ community, poor women, etc.).

None of us holds all the power to change the social generational default on our own, even in our own lives. No matter how much we consciously decide to do—*or not do*—we still live within the overarching systems and structures of our society, industries, and workplaces.

But the more control we can take back, the more times we fight back against gendered expectations, and the more we consciously work to write our own stories, the more momentum we can all build. And together we can create a new era of leadership—one that values women's wholeness, authenticity, and impact.

Glossary of Key Terms Used in This Book and Beyond

Allyship

The ongoing practice of using one's privilege or position to advocate for, support, and uplift people from marginalized identities. True allyship is active—it means speaking up, redistributing opportunity, and challenging inequity when you see it.

Benevolent Sexism

A form of sexism that appears subjectively positive—even flattering—on the surface, but actually reinforces traditional gender roles and contributes to gender inequality. It refers to attitudes, beliefs, or behaviors that idealize women in traditional roles (like being nurturing, pure, or in need of protection) and position them as weaker or dependent on men, often under the guise of kindness, chivalry, or admiration. It's sexism that *sounds nice* but still puts women in a box.

Conscious Choice

The act of intentionally making decisions based on your own values, desires, and priorities rather than following inherited scripts or external expectations. Living with conscious choice means designing your life and career on purpose rather than by default.

Default Scripts

Unspoken cultural rules or internalized narratives about how women should act, succeed, mother, or lead. Examples include "You should be grateful for the job," or "Good moms put themselves last." *Unscripted* invites women to question and rewrite these scripts.

Double Bind

A situation in which women are penalized no matter what they do. For example, being seen as too assertive if they lead strongly or too weak if they don't. The double bind often forces women to walk a narrow line between competence and likability with no "right" answer.

Emotional Labor

The often invisible work of managing others' emotions, smoothing tension, and maintaining harmony in relationships at home, at work, or in social settings. Women are disproportionately expected to take on this burden, often without recognition or support.

Gender Stereotypes

Widely held but oversimplified or generalized beliefs about the characteristics, roles, or behaviors typically associated with men or women. Gender stereotypes are assumptions or expectations about how people should think, feel, or act based solely on their gender and often reinforce rigid, binary roles that limit individual potential and reinforce inequality. They're the ideas we're taught about what women and men "should" be like.

Explicit Bias

Also known as Conscious Bias. Refers to the attitudes or beliefs we have about a person or group on a conscious level. These biases are intentional, deliberate, and often openly expressed. A person with explicit bias is aware of their preferences or prejudices and may act on them knowingly. It's when someone knows they have a bias and either justifies it or chooses not to challenge it.

Invisible Labor
All the unseen, behind-the-scenes effort that keeps life and work moving forward—from remembering birthdays to coordinating team schedules. This often overlaps with the mental load of emotional labor and disproportionately falls on women in both home and work environments.

Implicit Bias
Also known as Unconscious Bias. Refers to attitudes, stereotypes, or assumptions that affect our understanding, actions, and decisions in an unconscious way. These biases are automatic, unintentional, and often operate outside of our awareness, even if they contradict our stated values. It's when your brain makes snap judgments about people based on things like race, gender, age, or background without you even realizing it. It highlights the disconnect between what we say we believe and how we actually respond, often automatically, in real-world situations.

Likability Bias
The tendency to judge women more harshly than men when they exhibit traits associated with leadership—such as assertiveness, ambition, or confidence—because those traits conflict with traditional expectations of how women "should" behave. It's the double standard where women are expected to be warm, agreeable, and nurturing, and are penalized—socially or professionally—when they deviate from those norms. When a man is confident, he's respected. When a woman is confident, she's "bossy," "intimidating," or "unlikable."

Macroaggression

An overt, large-scale, or systemic act of discrimination or hostility toward a person or group based on their identity—such as race, gender, sexual orientation, or other marginalized traits. Macroaggressions are blatant, intentional, and often institutionalized actions or policies that harm, exclude, or devalue individuals. They can occur at the interpersonal, cultural, or structural level. It's the in-your-face version of bias—direct, obvious, and part of a larger pattern of inequality.

Mental Load

Refers to the invisible, ongoing, and often exhausting cognitive effort required to manage household responsibilities, relationships, and caregiving—including the planning, organizing, remembering, and decision-making that keeps everything running. Even in relationships that share physical tasks equally, the *mental load* is often disproportionately carried by women, contributing to burnout and emotional fatigue.

Microaggression

A subtle and often unintentional comment, action, or behavior that communicates a biased or derogatory message toward someone based on their identity—such as gender, race, age, or other marginalized traits. These are everyday slights, insults, or dismissive behaviors that reinforce stereotypes or reveal unconscious bias, especially toward people from historically marginalized groups. They're the "small" jabs or offhand remarks that sting and signal that someone doesn't fully see or respect you.

Misogyny

Hatred of, contempt for, or prejudice against women and girls. Misogyny refers to deeply ingrained distrust, dislike, or devaluation of women, and is often expressed through discrimination, belittlement, objectification, violence, or the undermining of women's power, voices, and autonomy. It's when women are treated as less valuable—or even as threats—simply because they are women.

Social Generational Default

The inherited set of beliefs, expectations, and roles passed down through generations—often unconsciously—that shape how women "should" behave at work, at home, and in society. These defaults are rooted in tradition and social conditioning and often conflict with women's authentic values and goals.

Interested in Going Deeper?

If you'd like to explore one-on-one coaching with Melissa or learn more about her retreats for women leaders, scan the QR code below. You'll find details, upcoming opportunities, and ways to connect. ♥

About the Author

Melissa Churchard Hannon is an executive coach, leadership development consultant, and mother of four with more than 25 years of experience. She helps women to understand the unconscious script they've inherited—and how to break free from the quiet conformity that keeps them overperforming and underfulfilled. Melissa supports leaders worldwide in creating lasting change. She is the founder of ALIGN LLC and serves on the board of Unlimited Possibilities, a nonprofit dedicated to global service and social impact. She lives on a small island off the coast of Maine with her family.

www.ingramcontent.com/pod-product-compliance
Lightning Source LLC
Chambersburg PA
CBHW051636120626
46551CB00014B/2110